MEDIEVALIA ET HUMANISTICA

MEDIEVALIA ET HUMANISTICA

STUDIES IN MEDIEVAL AND RENAISSANCE CULTURE

NEW SERIES: NUMBER 47

EDITED BY
REINHOLD F. GLEI (ARTICLES)
AND
MAIK GOTH (REVIEWS)
WITH THE EDITORIAL ASSISTANCE OF
CHRISTOPH SCHÜLKE

ROWMAN & LITTLEFIELD
Lanham • Boulder • New York • London

Published by Rowman & Littlefield
An imprint of The Rowman & Littlefield Publishing Group, Inc.
4501 Forbes Boulevard, Suite 200, Lanham, Maryland 20706
www.rowman.com

86-90 Paul Street, London EC2A 4NE

British Library Cataloguing in Publication Information Available

Library of Congress has catalogued this serial publication as follows:

Medievalia et humanistica, fasc. 1–jan. 1943–;
New ser. No 1– 1970–
Totowa, N.J. [etc.] Rowman & Littlefield [etc.]
no. 29 cm
Annual, 1943–
"Studies in medieval and renaissance culture."
Vols. for 1970–1972 issued by the Medieval and neo-Latin society;
1973– by the Medieval and Renaissance Society.
Key title: Medievalia et humanistica, ISSN 0076-6127.

ISBN 9781538157909 (cloth : alk. paper)
ISBN 9781538157916 (epub)

Library of Congress (8108)

∞™ The paper used in this publication meets the minimum requirements of
American National Standard for Information Sciences—Permanence of Paper
for Printed Library Materials, ANSI/NISO Z39.48-1992.

Contents

Review Notices

Editorial Note

Since 1970, this new series has sought to promote significant scholarship, criticism, and reviews within the fields of medieval and Renaissance studies. It has published articles from a variety of disciplines, and it has given attention to new directions in medieval and humanistic scholarship and to significant topics of general interest. This series has been particularly concerned with the exchange between specializations, and scholars of diverse approaches have complemented each other's efforts on questions of common interest.

Medievalia et Humanistica is sponsored by the Modern Language Association of America. Publication in the series is open to contributions from all sources, and the editorial board welcomes scholarly, critical, or interdisciplinary articles of significant interest on relevant material. Contributors are urged to communicate in a clear and concise style the larger implications and the material of their research, with documentation held to a minimum. Text, maps, illustrations, diagrams, and musical examples are published when they are essential to the argument of the article. In preparing and submitting manuscripts for consideration, potential contributors are advised to follow carefully the instructions given on pages ix and xi. Articles in English may be submitted to the editor Reinhold F. Glei or to any member of the editorial board. Books for review should be addressed to Christoph Schülke (Ruhr-Universität Bochum, Seminar für Klassische Philologie, GB 2 / 55, Universitätsstraße 150, 44780 Bochum, Germany). Inquiries concerning subscriptions should be addressed to the publisher:

Rowman & Littlefield
4501 Forbes Blvd, Suite 200
Lanham, MD 20706

Manuscript Submission Guidelines

Preparing Your Word File

- Double-space your file, except for extracts (lengthy quotes), which should be single-spaced with a line space above and below.
- Use only one space between sentences. Use tabs, not letter spaces, to indent text.
- Use the Notes feature of Word so the notes are embedded and autonumbered. Keep the superscript formatting in the notes section, without periods.

Style Matters

- Spell out numbers up to one hundred—both cardinals and ordinals (e.g., "twentieth century").
- Use American punctuation and spelling: commas and periods go inside closing quotation marks.
- Lowercase biblical, medieval. Capitalize Bible, Middle Ages, West, Western.
- Style for literary works includes Book of Acts, Genesis (book of the Bible), *Genesis A* (poem), Gospel of Matthew.
- Short quotations: Put short quotations in running text with translations in parentheses: "Ipsa autem nocte vidit mulier . . ." ("That very night his wife saw . . .").
- Long quotations: Set longer quotations off as extracts with the translation in brackets below. If the original text is poetry with half lines, use only one tab between each half line. Although the text will look uneven in your Word file, the tab will make the lines align exactly when typeset:

Cynewulf describes her as she sits on a throne while the Jews crowd around her:

> Þrungon þa on þreate   þær on þrymme bád
> in cynestole   casere mæg,
> geatolic guðcwen   golde gehyrsted.

[They crowded where the Caesar's kinswoman was waiting / in majesty upon a throne, / a magnificent battle-queen clad in gold] (329–31)

Sample Notes

Journal Article

[1] Melinda Shepard, "The Church in Eleventh-Century Europe," *Medieval Studies* 15, no. 1 (1993): 211–26.

Book

[2] Shepard, "Church in Eleventh-Century Europe," 223. Shepard notes other similarities as well. See also R. A. Potter, *Church and Medieval State* (Chicago: University of Chicago Press, 1979), 301.

Articles for Future Volumes

Articles may be submitted to the editor Reinhold F. Glei (mail to reinhold .glei@rub.de) or to any member of the editorial board:

David Bevington: bevi@uchicago.edu
Renate Blumenfeld-Kosinski: renatebk80@gmail.com
Robert Boenig: r-boenig@tamu.edu
Daniel Bornstein: dbornste@wustl.edu
Christopher Celenza: celenza@jhu.edu
Albrecht Classen: aclassen@email.arizona.edu
Jacques Dalarun: jacques.dalarun@irht.cnrs.fr
Peter Dembowski: pdembows@uchicago.edu
Yasmin Haskell: yasmin.haskell@uwa.edu.au
David Lines: d.a.lines@warwick.ac.uk
Richard Marsden: richard.marsden@nottingham.ac.uk
Adriano Prosperi: a.prosperi@sns.it
Francesco Stella: francesco.stella@unisi.it
Jan Ziolkowski: jmziolk@fas.harvard.edu

For inquiries concerning review articles and review notices please contact Maik Goth (mail to maik.goth@rub.de).

Prospective authors are encouraged to contact the editors at the earliest opportunity to receive any necessary advice. The length of the article depends on the material, but brief articles or notes normally are not considered. The entire manuscript should be typed, double-spaced, with ample margins; documentation should be held to a minimum. The articles need to be submitted via e-mail as Microsoft Word and PDF files. Notes, embedded and autonumbered using the Notes feature of Microsoft Word, should be prepared according to *The Chicago Manual of Style*, seventeenth edition (University of Chicago Press), should be double-spaced and numbered consecutively, and should appear at the end of the article. All quotations and references should be in finished form.

Preface

With the publication of volume 37 (2011) of *Medievalia et Humanistica*, Paul M. Clogan, who passed away in the summer of 2012, retired from editorship. The journal's international success and high reputation are due to his extraordinary erudition and ceaseless dedication. For this, the scholarly community is deeply indebted to him.

Since 2012 (volume 38), *M&H* has been in the hands of new editors: Reinhold Glei takes care of the articles, and Maik Goth is in charge of the reviews (beginning with volume 42). We endeavor to continue the well-proven approach of *M&H* and publish articles treating all facets of medieval and Renaissance culture: history, art, literature, music, science, philosophy, and so forth. This journal will continue to offer a platform for transdisciplinary and transepochal contributions, but we also welcome studies focusing on a single text or author. We intend to continue *M&H* as a well-established review journal and thus present new publications relevant to the journal's fields of interest.

At the end of 2017, our editorial assistant Nina Tomaszewski left the team to become a schoolteacher, and we want to express our warmest thanks to her for many years of excellent work. Christoph Schülke joined us as assistant in 2018.

Volume 47 presents four articles and seven book reviews, which cover various epochs, genres and discourses. In this issue, special focus lies on transnational and translingual perspectives, a paradigm that has gained momentum in recent years and hence features in *M&H* as well. We will develop the "trans-profile" of the journal further in the future.

As always, we are grateful to the staff of Rowman & Littlefield for their production of the annual volume.

Ruhr-Universität Bochum, December 2021

Medievalia et Humanistica, New Series, Number 47 (Reinhold F. Glei and Maik Goth, eds.), Rowman & Littlefield, 2022.

Johannes Reuchlin's Scaenica progymnasmata (Henno, *1497*) and Jacob Spiegel's Commentary (*1512*)

A Local and Transnational Project

JAN BLOEMENDAL

Abstract

Johannes Reuchlin's *Scaenica progymnasmata*, or *Henno*, (1497) was written in Heidelberg for local actors and a local audience. One of the pupil actors, Jacob Spiegel, wrote an extensive commentary on this play (1512). Thus, both phenomena (the play and the commentary) seem to be quite local. Yet the project betrays several transnational features: for instance, the writing of comedies, the theme of *Henno*, and the composition of Spiegel's commentary are all far from local. This article maps the transnational aspects of both the play and the commentary.

It is well-known that the Pforzheim jurist and philologist Johannes Reuchlin (1455–1522) wrote his comedy *Sergius, sive Capitis Caput* (Sergius, or the Head of the Head / Empty-Head) in 1496 or 1497 soon after he came to Heidelberg at the invitation of Johann von Dalberg (1445–1503), Prince-Bishop of Worms and chancellor of Elector Philip of the Palatinate.[1] The play was a vile satire, and therefore Dalberg, the central figure in the Heidelberg circle of humanists (the *Sodalitas litteraria Rhenana*, which was founded after the model of Italian *accademie*[2]) advised against a performance, and instead Reuchlin wrote his farce *Scaenica progymnasmata, hoc est Ludicra praeexercitamenta* (Preliminary Exercises on Stage, that is: Preparatory Training in the Form of a Play). It came to be known as *Henno* after the name of the farmer who was one of the characters and under the influence of the translation made by Hans

Medievalia et Humanistica, New Series, Number 47 (Reinhold F. Glei and Maik Goth, eds.), Rowman & Littlefield, 2022.

Sachs with that title.[3] It was performed on January 31, 1497 in Dalberg's house, and published in 1498 in Basel and in Strasbourg. The comedy has a "harmless" subject: the farmer Henno, who tricks his wife Elsa, is also being tricked in turn by his servant; the wife consults an astrologer, and the servant is accused and assisted by a lawyer who asks him to feign deafness and muteness by answering every question with merely one syllable "ble"; in turn, and when it was time to settle up, the lawyer is tricked by the same servant, again by saying "ble." only.

One of the pupil actors was Jacob Spiegel (1483/1484–ca. 1547), who had matriculated at Heidelberg University in 1496 to study dialectic and philosophy.[4] From 1500 to 1504, he studied Law in Freiburg, and would become a jurist and humanist known for his *Lexicon iuris civilis* (1538). In addition to his legal activities, he wrote a life of the early years of his uncle Jacob Wimpfeling (1450–1528), as well as commentaries on classical, patristic and contemporary authors, among which is a commentary on Reuchlin's *Henno* published in 1512 and reprinted in 1519. This farce and its commentary seem at first glance to be of a very local nature, as a humanist exercise in Dalberg's house, a celebratory event for humanistically inclined German scholars. An investigation of the case shows that local performances and publications may well have been marked by many transnational aspects, not the least since many of these scholars had studied in Italy, the *Sodalitas* was set up to keep the afterglow of Italianate humanism alive in the north, and the event had a similar purpose.

Heidelberg as a Cultural Hub

The geographical region where Reuchlin and Spiegel were active was also a *locus* for cultural exchange. The Upper Rhine, or the southwest of Holy Roman Empire, and particularly Heidelberg, was a center of international humanism.[5] Dalberg invited the Dutchman Rudolf Agricola (Roelof Huysman, 1444–1485) to teach in Heidelberg and join the *Sodalitas litteraria Rhenana*. Agricola had written a life of Petrarch, and had even taught at the University of Ferrara. In Heidelberg, where he resided only one year, 1484–1485, he taught *studia humanitatis*: grammar (i.e., the Latin language), rhetoric, poetry, history, and moral philosophy, through the reading of authors from classical antiquity.[6] Like other *tedesci* in the fifteenth century, Dalberg himself had also studied law and the humanities at Italian universities and took his degree of *doctor utriusque iuris* at the University of Ferrara.[7] After that, he traveled to Italian states and maintained contact with Italian humanists through correspondence. In these ways—study, travel, and correspondence—humanism crossed the Alps from the Italian peninsula to the German lands, all part of the Holy Roman Empire. He started an ecclesiastical career, and joined the court of the Elector of the Palatinate.[8] After the death of Agricola, Conrad Celtis (1459–1508) took the central role in the humanistic network around Dalberg. Trained in Heidelberg, Celtis traveled to Italy, Poland, and the northern parts of Germany and taught in Ingolstadt.[9] In 1495 he arrived in Heidelberg and established the *Sodalitas*.

Writing and Performing Latin Comedies

The writing of Latin plays itself was also a transnational affair. As we saw, *Henno* was written and performed in 1497. It was not the first play written in the German countries, but it was the first play to be written in Roman meter and in the tradition of the *fabula palliata*, the Roman comedy in Greek style. Earlier plays, such as Jacob Wimpfeling's *Stylpho* (1480) and Johannes Kerckmeister's *Codrus* (1485), were written in prose.[10] Comedies were previously imported from Italy.[11] Jacobus Dracontius (Jacob Trach), another member of the Heidelberg humanist circle and rector of the university, recognized this originality in a poem to Johann Richartshusen (who presided over the first performance and chose the actors) added to the *Scaenica progymnasmata*: "Huic vetus in nostris comoedia cede theatris, | Iam libeat soccum conspicere arte novum. | Nunc ex Germano dabitur spectare Poeta, | Mendicata prius / quae tulimus latio" (Old comedy, give way to this play in our theatres, now we wish to see a new art of drama. Now a poet from Germany gives us the opportunity to see a comedy, which formerly we borrowed from Italy). He is probably referring to Antonio Barzizza's *Cauteriaria* (1420/1425), which was brought from Italy (where he had studied) to Heidelberg by the professor of Latin Peter Luder between 1556 and 1560;[12] to Leonardo Bruni's *Poliscena* (1478) or Leon Battista Alberti's *Philodoxus fabula* (ca 1424); or to Ugolino Pisani's *Philogenia* (ca. 1476), which was translated and thus brought from Pavia to Germany by Albrecht von Eyb in 1459.[13] None of them, however, stood in the tradition of the *comoedia palliata* of Plautus and Terence. Yet, it is clear that the writing of Latin comedy had come to northern Europe in the footsteps of Italian humanism.

Latin drama in Germany undisputedly began with comedy, especially after the rediscovery of the Alexandrian grammarian Donatus's commentary on Terence's plays by Giovanni Aurispa in Mainz in 1433.[14]

Humanists read these comedies themselves and with their students, which gave Terence a special status, since they saw possibilities for moral instruction and Latin education. An important step in this development was Luder's Heidelberg inaugural lecture on July 15, 1456, in which he stressed the didactic value of these comedies that show people's characters and behavior.[15] However, in many contemporary editions of Terence with commentaries, with the exception of the Venice edition of 1479, the comedies were printed and treated as prose dialogues, as had been done in the Middle Ages, not as verses.[16] Another landmark for humanist Latin comedy was Celtis's 1501 edition of Hrotsvitha's medieval comedies after he discovered them in 1493/1494 and which he most likely discussed in the *Sodalitas*. His edition in turn inspired Kilian (Chilianus) von Mellerstadt's *Comoedia Dorotheae* (*Dorothee*, 1507); both Hrotsvitha and Von Mellerstadt wrote their plays in prose.[17]

Reuchlin's *Henno*

When Reuchlin wrote his *Henno*, we would also expect to find transnational traces in it, since it is written in the tradition of Roman comedy, especially that of Terence. Hundreds of editions of Terence's comedies were published at many places in Europe, often with the commentaries of the fourth-century grammarian Aelius Donatus, supplemented with commentaries by another ancient grammarian, Servius, the Italian philologist Johannes Calphurnius (Giovanni Calfurnio, 1443–1503), the French theologian and philologist Guido Juvenalis (Guy Jouenneaux, d. 1507), and the Flemish scholar and printer Jodocus Badius Ascensius (Josse Bade, 1562–1535).[18] Thus, the reception of Terence was a European phenomenon in itself, which started in Italy. Writing a Terentian comedy in the German lands is thus a revival of Terence as a means to transpose Italian humanism to the north of Europe and thus a self-definition of German humanists.[19] The prologue, the division into acts and scenes, and the *didascalium* and reminiscences in words and expressions in *Henno* all point to Terence. The same is true for the meter: the play is written in iambic trimeters, which was still unusual, especially when we take into account that most editions of Terence printed and treated his plays as dialogues in prose. In the prologue we find elements of an *argumentum* (summary) and remarks about the occasion, nature and intention of the play, exactly as Terence had done in his prologues. The play has neither a list of *dramatis personae* nor an epilogue, also in line with the ancient *palliata*. However, unlike in ancient comedy, it is not the *cantor* (Terence) or the *grex* (the entire group), but one single character, Greta, who is giving the usual *plaudite* formula: "Vobis salutem opto, huius et Comediae | Quibusque spectatoribus. Iam plaudite" (I wish you well, as well as all spectators of this comedy. Now clap your hands!).[20] Also the frequent use of stichomythia, which gives the comedy some rashness and lightness, aligns with ancient comedy. Some scenes can be connected to ancient ones. The dialogue between Henno and Dromo in the first scene resembles the dialogue between Simo and Sosia in Terence's *Andria*, and Elsa's monologue in act 3, scene 2 can be linked to the entrance of Euclio at the beginning of Plautus's *Aulularia*. As in ancient comedy, particularly that of Plautus, Reuchlin uses speaking or Cratylic names: Danista (giver of money, usurer), Dromo (runner) (directly derived from Roman comedy in the tradition of Greek Middle Comedy [i.e., of Menander]), Abra (the favorite), and Minos (the judge). However, Dromo is no longer the clever slave who serves his master,[21] but is a servant who climbs the social ladder by means of his tricks.

This characterization of Dromo also directs our attention to the transnational. Besides the cunning slave of Roman comedy, he fits the portrayal of the servant clown of the *Commedia dell'arte* and particularly has traits of the young servant Zanni, as well as his master Pantalone and Arlecchino.[22] Reuchlin will have become familiar with this kind of theater during his tours in Italy in 1482 and 1490/1491, although such theater was also already performed in German-speaking countries in the 1460s and 1480s.[23] Danista has traits of the character of Pantalone from the *Commedia dell'arte*, and Alcabicius resembles the Dottore.[24] Perhaps the chorus songs are inspired by the musical *intermezzi*, but the affinity of *Henno* with this Italian theater still has to be further researched.

The overall theme of *Henno* also crosses borders. The source of the main joke of *Henno*, the trick of saying "ble," is the French farce *Maître Pathelin*. The first edition of the French play was issued in 1474, and in the sixteenth century, some twenty editions were published. Tellingly, Philipp Melanchthon called *Henno* a "fabula Gallica."[25] However, besides some similarities, there are also many differences. The most significant similarities are in respect of the main theme of a lawyer who tricks a tailor: a shepherd who can't pay the tailor turns to the same lawyer, Pathelin. The lawyer advises him to answer every question with "bee," like sheep. When Pathelin asks the shepherd for his fee, the man responds with "bee." Reuchlin may have known the farce from his visit to Poitiers in 1481 and 1482 to study law.[26] According to Holstein, it is unlikely that Reuchlin knew the Latin translation by Alexander Connibert published in 1512 in Paris by the printer Guillaume Eustache and in 1543 by Simon Colinaeus in Paris for François Etienne.[27] In any case, the differences are more conspicuous than the similarities. *Pathelin* has two central scenes: a delirium scene and a dispute in court. The first is absent in *Henno*, and of the second, only rudiments are visible. Reuchlin would have omitted the most comical scenes.[28] Also the *dramatis personae* differ widely. In *Henno* the servant and the farmer couple are the main characters; in *Pathelin* it is the lawyer. The characterization of Elsa in *Henno* and Guillemette in *Pathelin* also differ: Elsa being a greedy, quarrelsome woman, Guillemette is an accomplice to her husband's deceit. Rather, the authors of *Henno* and *Pathelin* took comical motifs and molded them into a new play.

In this way, *Henno* was a very transnational play, in which four traditions are melded: classical comedy, medieval French farce, Renaissance Neo-Latin comedy from Italy, and the Italian *Commedia dell'arte*. Through this mixture, Reuchlin created a new type of play, putting a northern European stamp on the Italianate trace of Neo-Latin *Quattrocento* comedy, which in some cases barely differs from classical Latin comedy; see, e.g., Aeneas Silvius Piccolomini's *Chrysis*, which he wrote during his stay in Nuremberg in 1444.[29]

Henno itself also inspired others to write their comedies. In 's-Hertogenbosch, Georgius Macropedius (Joris van Lanckvelt, 1487–1558) wrote two farces, of which one has as its subject a farmer's wife (Aluta) who is tricked by two rogues, becomes drunk, and whose "drinking devil" is "exorcised" by a priest; in short, he substituted Reuchlin's French motifs with Dutch rhetoricians' elements. In the letter of dedication "Ad pueros bonarum litterarum studiosos," he wrote, stressing the novelty of Reuchlin's play and Reuchlin's (Capnion's) inspiring role:

Miratur quidam et ipse profecto doleo inter tot saeculi nostri viros doctissimos nullos Menandros, nullos Terentios reperiri, sed hoc scribendi genus paene ab ipsis Terentii aut certe Lucilii temporibus oblitteratum esse et antiquatum, quod tamen prae ceteris scriptorum generibus pluris merito foret aestimandum. Quid enim plus pueris ad eruditionem, plus adolescentibus ad honesta studia, plus provectioribus, immo omnibus in commune ad virtutem conducat quam docta comoedia? Quae recte ab aliis cotidianae vitae speculum, ab aliis imitatio vitae, speculum consuetudinis, imago veritatis, ab aliis ἰδιωτικῶν καὶ πολιτικῶν πραγμάτων ἀκίνδυνος περιοχὴ definitur. Consideravit hoc saeculi nostri et Germaniae decus Ioannes Capnion de omnibus litterarum studiis bene meritus, qui praeter hoc quod linguam Hebraicam primus Germaniae invexit, etiam collapsum prorsus artificium comicum primus instauravit. Is mihi primus (ut verum fatear) ansam scribendi dedit, is me primus excitavit. Si praeter eum hoc posteriori saeculo alii ante me scripserint, nescio. Hoc scio, quod alios non viderim.[30]

Macropedius also adopted Reuchlin's use of chorus songs set to music. Whether this was properly speaking a "transnational" affair can be questioned, since the Low Countries were part of the Holy Roman

Empire, and a cultural unity was felt through the conviction that Dutch was a dialect of German. In this case, boundary crossing is the crossing of nineteenth-century boundaries. But there is no doubt that it was a transregional affair.

If "crossing borders" includes language crossing, *Henno* was also a transnational text, translated into German or adapted in this language five times. The first translation was an anonymous one in a Hamburg manuscript, as a Shrovetide play, translated and performed shortly after 1500[31]; two were made by the Nuremberg *Meistersänger* Hans Sachs (1531)[32] and the poet Johann Betz (1546),[33] and one by the Berlin *rector scholae* Gregor Wagner (1547).[34] Also, the Lucerne New Year's play *Der kluge Knecht* is indebted to *Henno*, especially to the early 1500 translation *Comedia . . . traducta vulgariter.*[35] All of these translations take the comedy out of the school curriculum and highlight the folktale character.[36] Jacobus Rosefeldt's *Moschus* (1599), written on the occasion of a wedding, was partly indebted to Reuchlin's play and borrowed a few scenes from it almost literally.[37] In a more general sense, the use of choruses in *Henno* was also the inspiration for many Neo-Latin playwrights in the German lands and beyond for employing them.[38] The reasons for this success may have been the author's outstanding position in academia and society, the blossoming of humanism, sensed not only in Italy but now also in German-speaking countries.

Jacob Spiegel

As stated above, Jacob Spiegel was a pupil of Reuchlin and had been part of the cast in the play in 1497.[39] He was born in Schlettstadt (or Sélestat, in Alsace) in 1483 or 1484. After the death of his baker father, he was unable to remain at the famous Latin school of Schlettstadt for financial reasons, and was instead educated by his uncle Wimpfeling in Speyer[40] and then became a pupil of Reuchlin. He matriculated first at Heidelberg University (1496) to study dialectic and philosophy; the curriculum was old-fashioned, but he was able to join Dalberg's literary humanistic circle. After that, he had a career as a professor and was chancellor to Emperor Maximilian I.

The jurist and humanist Spiegel acted as a protector and literary agent for his uncle, but he also promoted other humanists. In turn, it was his kinship with Wimpfeling that paved the way to contact with the principal Alsatian humanists. Although he was best known for his *Lexicon iuris civilis*, he was also a commentator, mainly on contemporary Latin literary works, of which two were published in the same year: on

Reuchlin's *Scaenica progymnasmata* or *Henno* (1512, repr. 1519) and on the *Staurostichon* of Gianfrancesco Pico della Mirandola (1512).[41] He became acquainted with the Perugian poet Ricardo Bartolini, whose epic *Austriados* he edited and on which he commentated (1531),[42] as well as Giovanni Gioviniano Pontano's *De immanitate liber* (1519), and Antonius Panormita's *De dictis et factis Alphonsi* (1538). Through such commentaries he connected German to Italian humanism in the early years of or just before the Reformation, a connection that was promoted by the Italian humanist Pico, who had visited Maximilian in the years 1503 and 1505. Spiegel also edited Erasmus's hymn to Anna, the mother of Mary (1519) providing them with scholia. It is not clear why he chose only contemporary authors for his commentaries, with one exception: his commentary on the fourth-century Christian poet Prudentius's *Cathemerinon* (1520). Yet above all, he was a jurist whose *Lexicon* was one of the most important humanist contributions to civil law.

Spiegel's Commentary

In 1512, Spiegel published his lengthy Latin commentary on Reuchlin's *Henno* with Thomas Anshelm in Tübingen (*Ioannis Revchlin Phorcensis Scaenica progymnasmata, hoc est ludicra praeexercitamenta, cum explanatione Iacobi Spiegel Selestani.* Tubingae in aedibus Thomae Anshelmi Badensis mense octobri M.D.XII). It was reprinted seven years later (May 1519) when Spiegel published more commentaries on contemporary works. He gave this second edition the same title, but proudly added to his own name "Caes. Secret." (the emperor's secretary). The printer and publisher was the same Thomas Anshelm, who now resided in Hagenau, and was a special promotor of Reuchlin's works that he printed and sold.[43] Anshelm produced four editions of the *Scaenica progymnasmata* without annotations (1508, 1509, 1511, 1516) and two with Spiegel's commentary (1512, 1519).

Anshelm had also published a commentary on the other play by Reuchlin, *Sergius*. This commentary was written by the Graecist and rector of the Pforzheim Latin school Georg Simler (d. 1535/1536), who had himself studied at the Latin school of Schlettstadt.[44] Simler collaborated with Anshelm as a corrector, which resulted in editions, mostly with commentaries, including several works by Reuchlin, among which, the *Sergius* went to three editions: 1507, 1508 and 1513. Simler's commentary was probably also a source of inspiration for Spiegel's commentary on *Henno*.

Composing commentaries on contemporary plays was also a transnational affair and Simler's and Spiegel's commentaries on Reuchlin's plays were not alone, although they were two of the earliest examples. To name a few sixteenth-century examples: in Spain the master of grammar at the University of Toledo Alexius Vanegas published a commentary on Petrus Papaeus's comedy *Samarites*, both written and published in the Low Countries (1539, comm. 1542);[45] in London the priest and royal tutor John Palsgrave translated Guilielmus Gnapheus's *Acolastus* (1529), also written and published in the Low Countries, adding commentary (*The Comedy of Acolastus*, 1540); and in Paris the theologian and schoolmaster Gabriel Prateolus commented upon the same play (1554).[46]

Spiegel wrote a distinctive commentary, which he dedicated to the Tübingen theologian and jurist Jacob Lemp[47] and in which he included a short handwritten commentary by Reuchlin himself.[48] For the rest, it is a commentary that stresses grammatical and philological details, but also gives many *realia* from antiquity or his own time that are not necessary to understand the text.[49] The somewhat disparate character of Spiegel's commentary may be connected to the history of its genesis. As Rowan and Williams remark: "It appears that Spiegel had completed a commentary on the *Scaenica progymnasmata*, a Latin farce by Johann Reuchlin, before summer, 1511, though it would not be published until October, 1512. Spiegel had gradually built up a commentary on the play starting from grammatical glosses provided by Reuchlin himself for a manuscript prepared by Wimpfeling. The result was an accumulation of apparently random notes and comments on all aspects of contemporary knowledge" and "Over the years Spiegel had probably worked on his commentary to *Henno*. When he finally brought it to completion he had incorporated into it Reuchlin's own commentary without, however, identifying where it left off and his own began."[50] And also in other parts he often quotes passages from other works. He might well have done this from his own library. A list of his books happens to survive.[51] This *Index librorum Bibliothecae doctoris Iacobi Spiegelij Selestadiensis* provides a clear insight into the books he possessed. However, it was made in 1542, when he sold his books to Bishop Erasmus of Strasbourg—thirty years after he wrote his commentary on *Henno*. It therefore gives no secure indication of the books he owned or had at his disposal when writing the commentary. He may also have borrowed books from Reuchlin, of whose library we also have a clear idea, but with the same restriction.[52]

In his commentary, Spiegel does not so much explain Reuchlin's text but uses it as an occasion to give information about facts from antiquity and grammatical information. This is in contrast to Terence commentaries that gave grammatical, syntactical, or moral explanations.[53] An observation by Enenkel on another commentary by Spiegel also applies to this commentary: he does not compose it from his own experience but mediates knowledge through written tradition. In this way, he integrates the object of his commentary into the classical tradition[54] and connects the play to the classical Latin language, but also anchors it in contemporary humanism. The commentary steers the readers' views into the conviction that *Henno* is a learned, intertextually loaded literary text, with many legal implications.

At first sight, Spiegel's commentary seems to be local like *Henno* itself: the young, twelve or thirteen years old, Jacob was one of the actors in the first performance of the play, written and staged in Heidelberg, and as a twenty-eight or twenty-nine-year-old man, he wrote the commentary in the service of the printer Thomas Anshelm, Reuchlin's principal publisher. However, when we look at the commentary itself, another picture emerges. It is a hotchpotch of word-for-word quotations from earlier works, so that one could think of a complete lack of originality. These quotations stem from ancient authors, and therefore the impression arises that he had these authors to hand when he composed his annotations. One example may elucidate this:

Ingratum: Seneca de beneficiis: Ingratus est qui beneficium se accepisse negat, quod accepit. Ingratus est qui dissimulat, ingratus est qui non reddit, ingratissimus omnium qui est oblitus. Non possum praeterire quin subiiciam ad explodendam Aristotelicae ingratitudinis opinionem quantum Aristoteles Platoni magistro concesserit, quem a discipulo Aristotele in tradendis disciplinis neglectum aut saltem minus commendatum, cum et ab eo libere dissentiat, ac ignorantiae alicubi (ut quidam opinantur) arguat uulgo receptum est, quod ego aliter accipiendum existimo sicuti Macrobius et alii ueteres exponunt, neque enim uiginti annos dumtaxat academiae principem Platonem audiuit, sed eidem tantum tribuit atque concessit, ut eius quoque numini aram in templo construxerit, statuamque consecrauit, in qua descriptum esset, hunc esse illum quem probi omnes merito debeant et imitari et commendare, quod et Crinitus cuius ore iam loquimur in parthenicis suis attigit his uersibus: Haec illa est ara floribus redimita suaue olentibus. Quam gratus bene merenti statuit discipulus seni. Tituloque hoc testatus animum suum atque officium. Platonem probandum probe a probis, ab aliis nephas. Sic ille princeps et auctor egregius sapientiae tam diuturnae disciplinae et sacri muneris tulit dignum pro meritis tantis ab alumno suo praemium. Idem praeterea Aristoteles Platonis nomen sanctum atque diuinum uocitabat, egregiamque orationem de Platonis laude composuit, ut ab Olympiadoro proditum est. Licet quoque ex Codro intelligere quanti rursus Aristotelem fecerit diuinus ille Plato, cuius etiam praestantiam diuinauerat, quod uel eo potissimum argumento suspicari potest. Habebat Plato in academia magnam philosophantium cateruam, sed inter omnes eminebat Aristoteles, hunc Plato amabat, hunc contemplabatur, hoc gloriabatur. Certo die quum in auditorium Plato uenisset, et Aristotelem interesse non conspicaretur reliquis discipulis audientibus exclamauit intellectus non uenit, quasi omnes alii praeter Aristotelem crassi et obtusi essent ingenii, nec Platonem intelligerent. Post aliquot etiam dies cum idem accidisset Plato dixit abest philosophus ueritatis. Tertio circumferens oculos Plato et abesse Aristotelem cernens suspirauit dixitque κωφὸν τὸ ἀκροατήριον id est mutum auditorium, tanquam alii philosophantes prae Aristotele muta essent animalia.

Indignum igitur creditu est Aristotelem tam magnarum tam uerarum laudum immemorem umquam factum contendisse qui omni studio de se optime meritum praeceptorem semper redarguere et incommendatum praeterire, quod si ita esset profecto non minus quam Iasonis uel Thesei, uel Laomedontis, uel Paridis, uel Atheniensium, uel Syracusanorum, uel Alexandri magni, uel thebanorum, uel plurimum aliorum inter memorabilia deo hominibusque exosae ingratitudinis exempla, et haec quoque Aristotelis ingratitudo referenda notanda et detestenda esset in perpetuum. Qua culpa omnis nos decet discipulos carere. Meminerint discipuli praeceptoris sui bonitatem extollere, ne sub poenitendo (ut Beroaldus inquit) magistro militasse uideantur. Sunt praeterea ueluti parentes perpetua ueneratione obseruandi, quoniam erudiri et gigni paria sunt, cum alterum procreet animal, alterum faciat hominem. Non enim manus duas habere aut pedibus geminis proficisci, caeteraque eius modi quibus a brutis differimus hominem faciunt, sed rerum scientia et eloquentia quae nobiscum non nascuntur. Quantum autem debeamus honestis ac eruditis praeceptoribus abunde historiarum lectione assequimur. qua comperi ueteres principes et romanos et graecos suos praeceptores non modo summa et egregia obseruatione coluisse, sed honoribus etiam maximis atque dignitatibus persecutos fuisse. Nam parentibus et diis et praeceptoribus (ut inquit Plato) uix hercle pro merito illud uetus ἀντιπελαργεῖν obseruari potest, cum tanto muneri nullae satis gratiae referantur.

In this example, many authors from Greek and Roman antiquity and Italian humanists are quoted or mentioned, such as Plato (*Alcibiades* I, 135d7–e3) and Aristotle, but also Seneca, *De beneficiis* III, 1, 3; Antonius Urceus Codrus, *Orationes seu Sermones* (Bologna: Benedetto d'Ettore, 1502), Sermo VI, fol. xxv[v]–xxvi[r]; Philippus Beroaldus (Filippo Beroaldo), letter to Thomas Wolff, in *Hic subnotata continentur vita M. Catonis, Sextus Aurelius de vitis Caesarum, Benevenutus de eadem re, Philippi Beroaldi et Tomae Vuolphii Iunioris disceptatio de nomine imperatorio, epithoma rerum germanicarusque ad nostra tempora* (Strasburg: Thiergarten, 1505), unpaginated. However, the passage is fundamentally indebted to Pietro Crinito's (Pietro del Riccio Baldi, Petrus Crinitus, 1474–1507) compilation book *Commentarii de honesta disciplina* XXIV, 1 (Florence: Philippus de Giunta, 1504), fol. Oiii[v]:

Quantum Aristoteles Platoni magistro concesserit, ac versus in ara ab eo positi, et quod Magi etiam Platoni immolarunt, propter absolutum novies novenarium numerum. Receptum vulgo est Platonem, Academiae principem, fuisse a discipulo Aristotele in tradendis disciplinis neglectum, aut saltem minus commendatum, cum et ab eo libere dissentiat ac ignorantiae alicubi, ut quidam opinantur, arguat. Quod ego aliter accipiendum existimo, sicut Macrobius et alii veteres exponunt. Neque enim viginti annos dumtaxat in Academia Platonem audivit, sed eidem tantum tribuit atque concessit, ut eius quoque nomini aram in templo construxerit statuamque consecrarit, in qua descriptum esset : "Hunc esse ilium quem probi omnes merito debeant et imitari et commendare." Quod et nos in Parthenicis nostris attigimus his versibus: "Haec illast ara floribus redimita suaveolentibus, | Quam gratus benemerenti statuit discipulus seni, | Tituloque hoc testatus animum suum atque officium: | 'Platonem probandum probe a probis, ab aliis nefas.' | Sic ille princeps et auctor egregius sapientiae | Tam diuturnae disciplinae et sacri muneris tulit | Dignum pro meritis tantis ab alumno suo praemium." Idem praeterea Aristoteles Platonis nomen sanctum atque divinum vocitabat, egregiamque orationem de Platonis laude composuit, ut ab Olimpiodoro proditum est. Mitto autem nunc illud quod Annaeus Seneca de Magis Persarum tradit, quod hi quidem Platoni defuncto immolarunt quoniam suo natali decessisset, annumque unum supra octogesimum absolvisset, sine ulla prorsus additione vel deductione. Asserunt enim inter alia suae disciplinae dogmata, eum esse omnium perfectissimum numerum, quem novies novenum multiplicant, qua aetate Platonis philosophi fuisse interitum constat. Hinc Labeo Romanus theologus eumdem Platonem inter semideos, ut Herculem ac Romulum, referendum putavit.

For his commentary, Spiegel used many works by many prose authors from early Latin to his own times, often those who met his wish for providing information about the meaning of words and Roman society. Here a *liste raisonné* will be given that is not exhaustive. From early Latin he used, for instance, Varro's *De lingua Latina* and *De vita populi Romani*, and Cato's *De agri cultura*; from classical Latin, works such as several by Cicero, among which particularly the *Tusculanae disputationes, De natura deorum* and *Epistolae ad familiares*, and Livy's *Ab Vrbe condita*; from silver Latin, for example, Columella's work *De re rustica*, Macrobius's *Saturnalia*, Quintilian's *Institutio oratoria*, and Seneca's *Epistulae morales* and *Naturales quaestiones*; and from later Latin authors, such as Apuleius's *Metamorphoses* and *Apologia*, and the *Historiae Augustae scriptores*. He also quoted works by late-antique grammarians such as Festus's *De verborum significatu*, of which the sole extant manuscript was discovered in 1436 and published in Rome in 1475; Diomedes's *Ars grammatica* and Priscian's *Institutiones grammaticae*; as well as Firmicus Maternus's *Mathesis* and encyclopedias like Aulus Gellius's *Noctes Atticae*, Seneca Major's *Naturalis historia* and Nonius Marcellus's *De compendiosa doctrina*; but also works from Fathers of the Church, such as Jerome, in particular his *Epistolae*, Ambrosius and Augustine, from whose *Confessiones* and *De civitate Dei*, Spiegel took some quotations, as he did from Lactantius's *De opificio Dei* and his *Divinae institutiones*.

Of course, the jurist Spiegel also used legal works such as the *Codex Iustinianus*, the later additions of Ulpian's *Digesta* and works on canon law: Gregorius's *Decretales* and the *Decretum Gratiani*. This was also to be expected in a commentary on a play that partly deals with lawsuits and jurisprudence, but these sources were also quoted at passages that were less obvious.

Poets also abound in Spiegel's commentary, including the "usual suspects" such as the playwrights Plautus and Terence, the school authors Horace (his *Carmina* and his *Satires*), Ovid (particularly his *Metamorphoses*, *Heroides* and *Fasti*), and above all Virgil; but also works from "Silver Latinity," such as Martial's epigrams, Lucan's *Pharsalia* and Statius's *Thebais* were quoted.

However, Spiegel does not just quote the classical authors themselves, but he also consults and quotes commentators. He quotes Donatus's commentaries on Terence's plays—as well as his and/or Euanthius's *Excerpta de comoedia*—Servius's commentaries on Virgil, Pseudo-Asconius's commentary on Cicero, and Porphyrio's commentary on Horace. These are all commentators from antiquity. But he also knew and used—and here the transnational character of his commentary becomes very legible—the commentaries by the humanist and professor of rhetoric and poetry at Bologna university Filippo Beroaldo (Philippus Beroaldus, 1453–1505) on Apuleius's *Metamorphoses* (Bologna, 1500; Venice, 1501 and 1504),[55] on Cicero's *Tusculanae disputationes* (Bologna, 1499; Paris, 1500), and on Suetonius (Bologna, 1493; Venice, 1496, 1497, 1500, and 1506), as well as his annotations on Servius's commentary on Virgil (Florence, 1499; Paris, 1500–1501; Venice, 1512) and his *Proverbialis oratio* (Paris, 1505). Moreover, Spiegel quotes the commentated edition of Giovanni Battista Pio (Ioannes Baptista Pius, 1460–1540) on Plautus: *M. Plauti linguae Latinae principis comoediae XX* (Venice, 1511), an annotated edition of Pliny's letters by Giovanni Maria Cattaneo (Ioannes Maria Catanaeus, d. 1529), published in Venice in 1510. Finally, he quotes Cristoforo Zarotti's (fl. 1501–1550) commentary on Ovid's *Ibis* (Venice, 1501). It is revealing, that Spiegel had so many editions of Italian authors at hand, also very recent ones.

He also had other works by Italian authors at his disposal. One of the works he used most is Pietro Crinito's aforementioned compilation book *Commentarii de honesta disciplina* (Florence, 1504; Paris, 1508; Hagenau, 1510; Paris, 1510 and 1511).[56] Another source for his commentary was the Augustinian abbot Matthaeus Bossus's (Matteo Bosso, 1428–1502) *De veris ac salutaribus animi gaudiis* (Florence, 1491). Very often, Spiegel quotes Ambrogio Calepino's (Ambrosius Calepinus, ca. 1440–1510) famous *Dictionarium* (Reggio, 1502 and many other editions). This lexicon was so widely known that the name became a synonym for a dictionary or lexicon. Calepino gives meanings and offers quotations from classical and later authors; Spiegel frequently gives the same quotations.

The Bible is repeatedly quoted, too. For the Psalms, in some cases Spiegel used the *Quincuplex Psalterium* (Paris, 1509) by the French theologian and philologist Jacques Lefèvre d'Étaples (Jacobus Faber Stapulensis, 1455–1536).[57]

Greek authors also provided Spiegel with quotations, in most cases, however, in a Latin translation. Lefèvre d'Étaples, just mentioned, translated, commented on, paraphrased or wrote introductions to Aristotle's *Ethica Nicomachaea* (Paris, 1496), *De anima* (Leipzig, 1506), *Politica* (Paris, 1508 and 1512), and *Oeconomia* (Paris, 1506), which are quoted by Spiegel. For Plato's works he used the translations by Marsilio Ficino (Marsilius Ficinus, 1433–1499).

In other cases, he remained close to his relatives. He made use of the *Isidoneus Germanicus* (1496), in which his uncle Jacob Wimpfeling presented his humanistic pedagogical ideals and rejected scholasticism. Spiegel as a humanist endorsed his views of education: schooling should enable pupils to read pagan writers who were not immoral and Christian authors.

Final Remarks

Jacob Spiegel's commentary on Reuchlin's *Henno* is a compilation work without much originality, in the sense that most of his commentary consists of quotations from earlier works. However, the choice and combination of the authors quoted is original, as is the commentary itself. Both *Henno* and Spiegel's commentary are products of transnationalism, but for different reasons. The play itself fits in the tradition of Roman comedy and in comedy in the vein of Plautus and Terence, a tradition that came from *Quattrocento* Italy, whereas its main joke (saying "ble") is derived from a French farce, and some of the characters are modeled after characters in the Italian *commedia dell'arte*. The play in turn inspired other authors to make translations, adaptations, and original works. Spiegel's commentary is full of quotations from ancient authors, with their early modern interpreters and in their capacity as translators, editors, or commentators. Many of these interpreters lived, worked, or studied in Italy, the country where students who wished to advance in both secular and canon law attended classes. Thus the commentary is another substantiation of the important role lawyers played in the development of humanism on the Italian peninsula and the spread thereafter of humanism from Italy to the rest of Europe.[58] Moreover, it shows that books circulated widely and fast across Europe. In this way, the local enterprise of writing a Heidelberg commentary on a Heidelberg play turns out to be far more transnational (or transregional) than one could imagine. Transnationalism in this case is embodied by authors who as German students of law went to Italy and as mature publicists still remembered and used the works they had come to know in their formative years, since their educational tour also brought them in contact with Italian professors outside the strict domain of legal studies, and with their commentaries on classical authors. Therefore, it was not only a diatopical but also a diachronic phenomenon. In this case, this place (i.e., the city of Heidelberg), this time (i.e., the end of the fifteenth century), and these persons (i.e., the students of law) turned out to offer the ideal circumstances for writing such a Latin play and such a commentary. Reuchlin's play with Spiegel's commentary, although seemingly quite local, turns out to be a locus of literary transnationalism and transregionalism in many aspects: humanists traveling and studying in other regions and countries and adopting new literary forms, texts circulating, and publishers and printers distributing books. All of these elements were conflated into a distinctive commentary.

Notes

1. This article is written within the scope of the NWO-funded project: "TransLatin: The Transnational Impact of Latin Theatre from the Early Modern Netherlands, a Qualitative and Computational Analysis" (https://translatin.nl). A new edition of Reuchlin's *Henno* and the first scholarly edition of the commentary by Jacob Spiegel is being prepared by a seminar group of the Ruhr-University of Bochum under the supervision of the author of this article. The author would like to acknowledge the help of group members Theodor Lindken, Niklas Gutt, Gabriele Schwabe, and Wolfram Adam; the members of his TransLatin team Dinah Wouters, Jirsi Reinders, and Andrea Peverelli; and his colleagues James A. Parente Jr. and Nigel Smith for their valuable remarks. On Reuchlin's life, see, e.g., Ludwig Geiger, *Johann Reuchlin, sein Leben und seine Werke* (Leipzig: Duncker & Humblot, 1871); Heinz Scheible, "Johann Reuchlin of Pforzheim," in *Contemporaries of Erasmus: A Biographical Register of the Renaissance and Reformation*, eds. Peter G. Bietenholz and Thomas B. Deutscher, 3 vols. (Toronto, Buffalo, and London: University of Toronto Press, 1985–1987), 3:145–50; Stefan Rhein, "Johannes Reuchlin (1455–1522): Ein deutscher 'uomo universale,'" in *Humanismus im deutschen Südwesten: Biographische Profile*, ed. Paul Gerhard Schmidt (Stuttgart: Jan Thorbecke Verlag, 2000), 59–76. For a biography in English, see Franz Posset, *Johann Reuchlin (1455–1522): A Theological Biography* (Berlin and Boston: Walter de Gruyter, 2015).
2. On Dalberg, see, for instance, Bietenholz and Deutscher, *Contemporaries*, 1:374 (Ilse Guenther); *Der Wormser Bischof Johann von Dalberg (1482–1503) und seine Zeit*, ed. Gerold Bönnen and Burkard Keilmann, Quellen und Abhandlungen

zur mittelrheinischen Kirchengeschichte 117 (Mainz: Selbstverlag der Gesellschaft für mittelrheinische Kirchengeschichte, 2005), esp. Peter Walter, "'Inter nostrae tempestatis pontifices facile doctissimus': Der Wormser Bischof Johannes von Dalberg und der Humanismus," 89–152. On the *Sodalitas* and its Italian inspiration, see Tibor Klaniczay, "Celtis und die Sodalitas litteraria per Germaniam," in *Respublica Guelpherbytana: Wolfenbütteler Beiträge zur Renaissance- und Barockforschung: Festschrift für Paul Raabe*, ed. August Buck and Martin Bircher, Chloe: Beihefte zum Daphnis 6 (Amsterdam: Rodopi, 1987), 79–105, esp. 82–83.

3. Modern editions in Hugo Holstein, *Johann Reuchlins Komödien: Ein Beitrag zur Geschichte des lateinischen Schuldramas* (Halle a. S.: Verlag der Buchhandlung des Waisenhauses, 1888), 11–34; Johannes Reuchlin, *Henno: Lateinisch/Deutsch*, ed. Harry Schnur (Stuttgart: Reclam, 1970).

4. On Spiegel, see, e.g., Thomas Burger, *Jakob Spiegel: Ein humanistischer Jurist des 16. Jahrhunderts* (Augsburg: Werner Blasaditsch, 1973) (diss., Freiburg im Breisgau); Bietenholz and Deutscher, *Contemporaries*, 3:270–72 (Miriam U. Chrisman); Karl Heinz Burmeister, "Spiegel (de Speculis, Specularis, Spegellius, Spi-; auch Wimpfeling Junior), Jakob," in *Deutscher Humanismus 1480–1520: Verfasserlexikon*, ed. Franz Joseph Worstbrock, 3 vols. (Berlin, etc.: De Gruyter, 2006–2015), vol. 2, cols. 936–48. On Spiegel's relationship to Reuchlin, see Burger, *Jakob Spiegel*, 80–82; on his library, Burmeister, "Die Bibliothek des Jakob Spiegel," in *Das Verhältnis der Humanisten zum Buch*, ed. Fritz Krafft and Dieter Wuttke (Boppart: Harald Boldt Verlag, 1977), 163–83.

5. See, for instance, *Humanismus im deutschen Südwesten: Akten des gemeinsam mit dem Verein für Kunst und Altertum in Ulm und Oberschwaben und dem Stadtarchiv-Haus der Stadtgeschichte Ulm am 25./26. Oktober 2013 veranstalteten Symposions im Schwörhaus Ulm*, ed. Franz Fuchs and Gudrun Litz, Pirckheimer Jahrbuch 29 (Wiesbaden: Harrassowitz, 2015); and *Humanismus im deutschen Südwesten: Biographische Profile*, ed. Schmidt (as in n. 1).

6. See on him, for instance, *Rodolphus Agricola Phrisius (1444–1485): Proceedings of the International Conference at the University of Groningen 28–30 October 1985*, ed. Fokke Akkerman and Arjo Vanderjagt (Leiden: Brill, 1988) and Rudolph Agricola, *Six Lives and Erasmus's Testimonies*, ed. and trans. ann. Fokke Akkerman (Assen: Van Gorcum, 2012).

7. See on the humanistic schooling of German students at Italian universities Agostino Sottili, "Die humanistische Ausbildung deutscher Studenten an den italienischen Universitäten im 15. Jahrhundert: Johannes Löffelholz und Rudolf Agricola in Padua, Pavia und Ferrara," in *Die Welt im Augenspiegel: Johannes Reuchlin und seine Welt*, ed. Daniela Hacke and Bernd Roeck, Pforzheimer Reuchlinschriften 8 (Stuttgart: Jan Thorbecke Verlag, 2002), 67–132.

8. On Dalberg, see, for instance, Peter Walter, "Johannes von Dalberg und der Humanismus," in *1495—Kaiser, Reich, Reformen: Der Reichstag zu Worms: Katalog zur Ausstellung des Landeshauptarchivs Koblenz in Verbindung mit der Stadt Worms* (Koblenz: Landesarchivverwaltung Rheinland-Pfalz, 1995), 139–71; Bönnen and Keilmann, *Der Wormser Bischof Johann von Dalberg (1482–1503)*, particularly the chapter by Peter Walter, "'Inter nostrae tempestatis Pontifices facile doctissimus': Der Wormser Bischof Johannes von Dalberg und der Humanismus," 89–152; Dieter Mertens, "Bischof Johann von Dalberg (1455–1503) und der deutsche Humanismus," in *Ritteradel im Alten Reich: Die Kämmerer von Worms genannt von Dalberg*, ed. Kurt Andermann (Epfendorf: Bibliotheca academica Verlag, 2009), 35–50.

9. On him, see Leo W. Spitz, *Conrad Celtis, the German Arch-humanist* (Cambridge, MA: Harvard University Press, 1957). See also Gerald Dörner, *Reuchlin und Italien*, Pforzheimer Reuchlinschriften 7 (Stuttgart: Jan Thorbecke Verlag, 1999).

10. Editions in Jakob Wimpfeling, *Stylpho: Lateinisch/Deutsch*, ed. Harry C. Schnur (Stuttgart: Reclam, 1971); Johann Kerckmeister, *Codrus: Ein neulateinisches Drama aus dem Jahre 1485*, ed. Lothar Mundt (Berlin and New York: de Gruyter, 1969).

11. See Cora Dietl, "Neo-Latin Humanist and Protestant Drama in Germany," in *Neo-Latin Drama and Theatre in Early Modern Europe*, ed. Jan Bloemendal and Howard B. Norland, Drama and Theatre in Early Modern Europe 3 (Leiden and Boston: Brill, 2013), 103–83, esp. 105. See also Werner Röcke, "Das Lachen der Gelehrten: Reuchlin und die humanistische Komödie des späten 15. Jahrhunderts," Hacke and Roeck, *Die Welt im Augenspiegel*, 147–60, and Alessandro Perosa, *Teatro umanistico* (Milan: Nuova Accademia, 1965).

12. On Luder's study in Italy and return to Germany, see Rudolf Kettemann, "Peter Luder (um 1415–1472): Die Anfänge der humanistischen Studien in Deutschland," in Schmidt, *Humanisten im deutschen Südwesten*, 13–34, esp. 13–14, and W. Wattenbach, "Peter Luder, der erste humanistische Lehrer in Heidelberg," *Zeitschrift für die Geschichte des Oberrheins* 22 (1859), 33–127. On Antonio Barzissa (Antonius Barzicius or Buzarius) and his *Cauteraria*, see Paul Bahlmann, *Die Erneuerer des antiken Dramas und ihre ersten dramatischen Versuche 1314–1478* (Münster: Regenburg'sche Buchhandlung, 1896), 47–48; a study and an edition can be found in Ernst W. Beutler, "Die Comoedia Cauteriaria des Antonio Barzizza," *Forschungen und Texte zur frühhumanistischen Komödie* (Hamburg: Selbstverlag der Staats- und Universitäts-Bibliothek;, 1927), 1–77 and 155–79.

13. Cora Dietl, *Die Dramen Jacob Lochers und die frühe Humanistenbühne im süddeutschen Raum* (Berlin and New York: de Gruyter, 2005), 169. Eyb translated the play into German in 1472/1473, see Paul Bahlmann, *Die Erneuerer des antiken Dramas und ihre ersten dramatischen Versuche 1314–1478* (Münster: Regenburg'sche Buchhandlung, 1896), 32–36, and Sven Limbeck, "Theorie und Praxis des Übersetzens im deutschen Humanismus: Albrecht von Eybs Übersetzung der 'Philogenia' des Ugolino Pisani" (doctoral thesis, Freiburg im Breisgau, 2000). A modern edition of Alberti's *Philodoxus* can be found in *Humanist Comedies*, ed. and trans. Gary R. Grund, I Tatti Renaissance Library 19 (Cambridge, MA, and London: Harvard University Press, 2005), 70–169, and of Pisani's *Philogenia*, ibid., 170–283; see also Bahlmann, *o.c.*, 27–30; on Bruni's *Polyscena*, see Bahlmann, *Die Erneuerer des antiken Dramas*, 20–23.

14. Dietl, *Die Dramen Lochers*, 20, referring to Max Hermann, "Terenz in Deutschland bis zum Ausgang des 16. Jahrhunderts: Ein Überblick," *Mitteilungen der Gesellschaft für deutsche Erziehungs- und Schulgeschichte* 3 (1893), 1–28, esp. 9.

15. Dietl, *Die Dramen Lochers*. The text of this programmatic oration on humanism can be found in Walter Wattenbach, "Peter Luder, der erste humanistische Lehrer in Heidelberg," *Zeitschrift für die Geschichte des Oberrheins* 22 (1869), 33–127, esp. 100–10. On the lecture, see, e.g., Wilfried Barner, "'Studia toto amplectenda pectore': Peter Luders Heidelberger Programmrede vom Jahre 1456," in *Pioniere, Schulen, Pluralismus: Studien zu Geschichte und Theorie der Literaturwissenschaft*, ed. Barner (Tübingen: Max Niemeyer Verlag, 1997), 3–21.

16. Publius Terentus Afer, *Comoediae* (Venice: Nicolaus Girardengus, 1479), containing the texts of the comedies and the commentaries by Aelius Donatus and Johannes Calphurnius, as well as the Life of Terence and Euanthius's *De fabula*.
17. The latter play was adapted into Danish ca. 1531 by Christiern Hansen. An incomplete version is preserved a manuscript containing four Neo-Latin dramas, probably performed at the humanist school in Odense.
18. See Jan Bloemendal, "In the Shadow of Donatus: Observations on Terence and Some of His Early Modern Commentators," in *Neo-Latin Commentaries and the Management of Knowledge in the Late Middle Ages and the Early Modern Period (1400–1700)*, ed. Karl Enenkel and Henk Nellen, Supplementa Humanistica Lovaniensia 33 (Louvain: Leuven University Press, 2013), 295–323.
19. See also James A. Parente Jr., "Empowering Readers: Humanism, Politics, and Money in Early Modern German Drama," *The Harvest of Humanism in Central Europe: Essays in Honor of Lewis W. Spitz*, ed. Manfred P. Fleischer (St. Louis: Concordia Press, 1992), 263–80, who makes a plea for studying humanist drama not only as a literary but also as a social phenomenon.
20. Otto Brunken, "1498: Johannes Reuchlin (1455–1522): Scaenica Progymnasmata: Hoc est: Ludicra Preexercitamenta. Basel 1498," in *Handbuch zur Kinder- und Jugendliteratur: Vom Beginn des Buchdrucks bis 1570*, ed. Theodor Brüggemann and Otto Brunken (Stuttgart: J.B. Metzler, 1987), cols. 331–44, 1163–67, esp. col. 338, assumes that the last words were part of the action and spoken to Dromo and Abra, but clearly the spectators are addressed.
21. See George E. Duckworth, *The Nature of Roman Comedy*, 5th ed. (Princeton, NJ: Princeton University Press, 1971 [1st ed. 1951]), 249–53.
22. See, for instance, Jane O. Newman, "Textuality versus Performativity in Neo-Latin Drama: Johannes Reuchlin's Henno," *Theatre Journal* 38 (1986): 259–74; she refers to, *inter alia*, Walter Hinck, *Das deutsche Lustspiel des 17. und 18. Jahrhunderts und die Italienische Komödie: Commedia dell'arte und Theatre Italien* (Stuttgart: Metzler, 1965) and Wolfgang Theile, "Commedia dell'arte," Rudolf Rieks, Wolfgang Theile, and Dieter Wuttke, *Commedia dell'arte: Harlekin auf den Bühnen Europas* (Bamberg: Bayerische Verlagsanstalt, 1981), 11–24. See also Kenneth Richards, "The Commedia dell'Arte Acting Companies," in *The Routledge Companion to Commedia dell'Arte*, ed. Judith Chaffe and Olly Crick (London and New York: Routledge, 2015), 43–52; M. A. Katritzky, "German-Speaking Countries," *Commedia dell'Arte in Context*, ed. Christopher B. Balme, Piermario Vescovo, and Daniele Vianello (Cambridge: Cambridge University Press, 2018), 98–105.
23. Katritzky, 'German-Speaking Countries,' 98–99.
24. Brunken, "Johannes Reuchlin", col. 342.
25. Philipp Melanchthon, "De Capnione Phorcensi,'" *Epistolae, praefationes, consilia, iudicia, schedae academicae*, ed. Karl Gottlieb Bretschneider, Corpus Reformatorum 11 (Halle: Schwetschke, 1843), cols. 999–1010, esp. 1004–5: "Ibi comoediam scripsit, Capitis caput, plenam nigri salis et acerbitatis adversus monachum, qui eius vitae insidiatus erat. Ibi et alteram comoediam edidit fabulam gallicam, plenam candidi salis, in qua forensia sophismata praecipue taxat. Hanc narrabat hac occasione scriptam et actam esse. Cum alteram de monacho scripsisset, fama sparsa est de agenda comoedia, quod illo tempore inusitatum erat. Dalburgius lecta illi monachi insectatione dissuasit editionem et actionem . . . Intellexit periculum Capnio, et hanc comoediam occultavit. Interea tamen quia flagitabatur actio, alteram dulcem fabellam edit et repraesentari ab ingeniosis

adolescentibus, quorum ibi extant nomina, curat"; see Holstein, *Reuchlins Komödien*, 41n. See also the German translation of the oration by Matthias Dall'Asta, which is to be found in *Melanchthon deutsch*, vol. 1: *Schule und Universität, Philosophie, Geschichte und Politik*, ed. Michael Beyer, Stefan Rhein, and Günther Wartenberg (Leipzig: Evangelische Verlagsanstalt, 2011 [= 1997]), 183–201, esp. 190–91.

26. Holstein, *Reuchlins Komödien*, 43.

27. Holstein, *Reuchlins Komödien*, 44: *Pathelin, comoedia nova, quae Veterator inscribitur, alias Pathelinus, ex peculiari lingua in Romanum traducta eloquium, per Alex.* Connibertum Parisiis, Guillaume Eustache, 1512; and *Patelinus. Nova Comoedia, aliàs Veterator, è vulgari lingua in Latinâ traducta per Alexandrum Conibertum LL. doctorem, et nuper quàm diligentissimè recognita; et conferenti cum veteri exemplari planè noua, hoc est longè tersior latinisque auribus gratior videatur.* Imprimebat Simon Colinaeus Francisco Stephano. 1543. A modern edition in Walter Frunz, "Comoedia nova que Veterator inscribitur alias Pathelinus ex peculiari lingua in Romanum traducta eloquium: Die neulateinische Bearbeitung des 'Maistre Pierre Pathelin'" (diss., Zürich, 1977).

28. Brunken, "Johannes Reuchlin," cols. 340–41.

29. See, e.g., Emily O'Brien, "Aeneas Silvius Piccolomini's *Chrysis*: Prurient Pastime or Something More?," *Modern Language Notes* 124 (2009), 111–38.

30. Georgius Macropedius, *Comicarum fabularum duae, Rebelles uidelicet et Aluta: pueris tum ad eruditionem, tum ad pios mores non parum profuturae* (Buscoducis: Gerardus Hatardus, 1535). *Aluta*, a farce on a farmer's wife who is tricked by two rogues, probably was written around 1515. See also Georgius Macropedius, *Rebelles und Aluta*, ed. Johannes Bolte (Berlin: Weidmannsche Buchhandlung, 1897), 3–4 and Georgius Macropedius, *Aluta*, ed. Jan Bloemendal and Jan W. Steenbeek (Voorthuizen: Florivallis, 1997 [1st ed. 1995]), 38. The definitions of comedy stem from Donatus, *De comoedia* 5, 5 and 5, 1; the definition as "cotidianae vitae speculum" is ascribed to Cicero (cf. *S. Rosc.* 47); for the definition of comedy as "imitatio vitae . . . veritatis," cf. Cic., *Rep.* IV, 11.

31. *Comedia Jo: Reuch: traducta vulgariter.* See Beutler, "Eine unbekannte deutsche Bearbeitung von Reuchlins Henno," in: *id., Forschungen und Texte zur frühhumanistischen Komödie* (Hamburg: Selbstverlag der Staats- und Universitäts-Bibliothek;, 1927), 103–48 and 205–24, and Stephan Rhein, "Reuchliniana III: Ergänzungen," *Johannes Reuchlin (1455–1522): Nachdruck der 1955 von Manfred Krebs herausgegebenen Festgabe*, ed. Hermann Kling and Stefan Rhein, Pforzheimer Reuchlinschriften 4 (Sigmaringen: Thorbecke, 1994), 303–25, esp. 309–10.

32. *Eine Comedi, mit X Personen zu Recidiern, Doctor Reuchlins im Latein gemacht, der Henno.* Modern edition in *Henno: Bauernkomödie: Latein von Johannes Reuchlin, Deutsch von Hans Sachs*, ed. Karl Holl ([Konstanz: Reuss and Itta], 1922) and in Hans Sachs, *Werke*, ed. Adelbert von Keller (Stuttgart: Bibliothek des litterarischen Vereins, 1873), 7:124–53.

33. *Ein Comedi, die sich wol dem Sprichwort vergleicht, so gesagt wirt. Ein betrug, betreugt den andern, dauon diese Comedi* (Nuremberg: G. Wachter, 1546).

34. *Ein hübsche deutsche Comedi, die da leret das Vntrew seinen eigen Herrn schlecht* (Frankfurt an der Oder: Nicolaus Wolrab, 1547).

35. See Hans-Gert Roloff, "Sozialkritik und Komödie: Reuchlin als Komödienautor," in *Kleine Schriften zur Literatur des 16. Jahrhunderts*, ed. Christiane Caemmerer a.o., Chloe: Beihefte zum Daphnis 35 (Leiden: Brill, 2003), 119–139, esp. 119; Brunken, "Johannes Reuchlin," col. 343; Hans Wuhrmann, *Das*

Luzerner Spiel vom Klugen Knecht: Ein Beitrag zur Erforschung des schweizerischen Dramas im frühen 16. Jahrhundert, (doctoral. thesis, Zurich, 1975). A modern edition by Hans Wuhrmann in *Fünf Komödien des 16. Jahrhunderts: Anonymus: Der kluge Knecht (um 1505); Hans Salat: Der verlorene Sohn (1537); Zacharias Bletz: Die missratenen Söhne (1546); Hans Rudolf Manuel: Das Weinspiel (1548); Tobias Stimmer: Comedia von zwei jungen Eheleuten (1580)*, ed. Walter Haas a.o. (Bern and Berlin: Paul Haupt, 1989), 15–60.

36. Brunken, "Johannes Reuchlin," col. 343.
37. On Rosefeldt, see *Allgemeine Deutsche Biographie* 29 (1889), 187–88 (Johannes Bolte) https://www.deutsche-biographie.de/pnd129299456.html (accessed January 31, 2021). Moschus (another name for Moses) is the merchant of the Jews. Rosefeldt was inspired not only by Neo-Latin plays, particularly Reuchlin's *Henno*, but also by English drama, especially Shakespeare's *Merchant of Venice* (esp. in the court scene), which he probably knew through English strolling players in Germany (Bolte, "Jacobus Rosefeldt").
38. Volker Janning, *Der Chor im neulateinischen Drama: Formen und Funktionen*, Symbolische Kommunikation undgesellschaftliche Wertesysteme: Schriftenreihe des Sonderforschungsbereichs 496 7 (Münster: Rhema, 2005), 37.
39. On Spiegel, see the references given above, n. 5.
40. On Wimpfeling, see *Contemporaries*, 3:447–59 (Barbara Könneker). On Spiegel and Wimpfeling, see Burger, *Jakob Spiegel*, 89–92.
41. On Spiegel as a commentator, see Karl Enenkel, "Kommentare als multivalente Wissenssammlungen: Das 'Fürstenspiegel'-Kommentarwerk Antonio Beccadellis (*De dictis et factis Alphonsi Regis Aragonum*, 144), Enea Silvio Piccolominis (1458) und Jakob Spiegels (1537)," in *Neo-Latin Commentaries and the Management of Knowledge*, ed. Enenkel and Nellen, 79–138, esp. 122–35. On the historical and political context of the commentary on Reuchlin, see Steven Rowan and Gerhild Scholz Williams, "Jacob Spiegel on Gianfrancesco Pico and Reuchlin: Poetry, Scholarship and Politics in Germany in 1512," *Bibliothèque d'humanisme et renaissance: Travaux et documents* 44 (Geneva: Droz, 1982), 291–305, esp. 301–05.
42. See Gerhild Scholz Williams, "Vergil in Wien: Bartholinis Austriados Libri XII und Jakob Spiegels Kommentar," *Acta Conventus Neo-Latini Guelpherbytani: Proceedings of the Sixth International Congress of Neo-Latin Studies, Wolfenbüttel, 12 August to 16 August 1985*, ed. Stella P. Revard, Fidel Rädle, and Mario A. Di Cesare, Medieval and Renaissance Texts and Studies 53 (Binghamton, NY: Medieval and Renaissance Texts and Studies, 1980), 171–80. On Bartolini, see *Dizionario biografico degli Italiani*, s.v. "Bartolini, Ricardo."
43. Holstein, *Reuchlins Komödien*, 56–57; Isabel Greschat, "Reuchlin und sein Drucker Thomas Anshelm," *Johannes Reuchlins Bibliothek Gestern und Heute: Schätze und Schicksal einer Büchersammlung der Renaissance*, ed. Matthias Dall'Asta, Gerald Dörner, and Isabel Greschat (Heidelberg etc.: Verlag Regionalkultur, 2007), 31–41; Peter Amelung, "Reuchlin und die Drucker seiner Zeit," *Schwäbische Heimat* 2 (1972): 168–77; Hildegard Alberts, "Reuchlins Drucker, Thomas Anshelm: Mit besonderer Berücksichtigung seiner Pforzheimer Presse," *Johannes Reuchlin 1455–1522: Festgabe seiner Vaterstadt Pforzheim zur 500. Wiederkehr seines Geburtstages*, ed. Manfred Krebs (Pforzheim: Selbstverlag der Stadt Pforzheim, 1955 [repr. Sigmaringen: Thorbecke, 1994]), 205–65. The VD16 lists some thirty issues of Reuchlin works printed by Anshelm, of which seven were translations or editions.
44. On him, see *Contemporaries*, 3:253 (Ilse Guenther); Reinhard Pohlke, "Simler, Georg." *Verfasserlexikon*, ed. Worstbrock, vol. 2, cols. 911–19. In

1496–1497 Simler studied in Heidelberg, where he probably met Reuchlin, who recommended him for the position of rector of the Pforzheim Latin school; on his commentary on *Sergius*, see Pohlke, "Simler, Georg," col. 916.

45. Modern edition in Daniel Nodes, *Parables on a Roman Comic Stage: Samarites—Comoedia de Samaritano evangelico (1539) by Petrus Papeus: Together with the Commentary of Alexius Vanegas of Toledo (1542)*, Drama and Theatre in Early Modern Europe 7 (Leiden and Boston: Brill, 2017). Vanegas wrote a grammatical and theological commentary.

46. *Johannis Palsgravii Londoniensis Ecphrasis Anglica in Comoediam Acolasti: The Comedye of Acolastus translated into oure englysshe tongue* (London: Thomas Berthelet, 1540); modern edition by P. L. Carver (London: Early English Text Society, 1937). *Comoedia Acolasti, authore Gulielmo Gnaphaeo, Gabrielis Prateoli Marcosii commentariis illustrata* (Paris: The Widow of Mauricius à Porta, 1554). Prateolus treats *Acolastus* as a Terentian play, with a commentary that resembles that of the Terence-editions with commentaries by, among others, Donatus. See Jan Bloemendal, "Une comédie biblique des Pays-Bas publiée en France: L'édition commentée de *l 'Acolastus* (Gulielmus Gnapheus, 1529) par Gabriel Dupreau (Paris, 1554)," *Le théâtre néo-latin en France au XVIe siècle: Études et anthologie*, ed. Mathieu Ferrand and Sylvia Laigneau-Fontaine, Cahiers d'Humanisme et Renaissance 170 (Geneva: Droz, 2021), 159–71.

47. On him, see *Allgemeine deutsche Biographie* 18, 239–40 (Julius Hartmann).

48. Holstein, *Reuchlins Komödien*, 60; Holstein published the text of this commentary on 97–106. The manuscript, which Wimpfeling gave to his nephew Jacob Sturm, is preserved in the University Library of Uppsala (Codex Uppsala, UB, C 687, fol. 8ʳ–21ᵛ), see on it: Margarete Andersson-Schmitt, Håkan Hallberg, and Monica Hedlund, *Mittelalterliche Handschriften der Universitätsbibliothek Uppsala: Katalog über die C-Sammlung*, vol. 6: *Handschriften C 551–935*, Acta Bibliothecae R. Universitatis Upsaliensis XXVI, 6 (Stockholm: Almqvist & Wiksell International, 1993), 279–96. It's a question whether the manuscript was copied by Wimpfeling, or an original Reuchlin handwriting, see Jan-Hendryk Boer, *Unerwartete Absichten: Genealogie des Reuchlinkonflikts*, Spätmittelalter, Humanismus, Reformation / Studies in the Late Middle Ages, Humanism, and the Reformation 94 (Tübingen: Mohr-Siebeck, 2016), 600, n. 145.

49. This character of the commentary as a *Fundgrube* of knowledge for linguistic and cultural knowledge of antiquity is enhanced by the inclusion of a "Dictionum index"; such a presentation gives the *Scaenica progymnasmata* a kind of canonical status.

50. Rowan and Williams, "Jacob Spiegel on G. Pico and Reuchlin," 292 and 302.

51. Alfons Semler, "Die Bibliothek des Humanisten Jakob Spiegel," *Zeitschrift für die Geschichte des Oberrheins* N.F. 32 (1917), 85–97; Burmeister, "Die Bibliothek des Jakob Spiegel."

52. See Greschat, Dall'Asta, and Dörner, *Johannes Reuchlins Bibliothek*; Karl Christ, *Die Bibliothek Reuchlins in Pforzheim*, Beiheft zum Zentralblatt für Bibliothekswesen (Leipzig: Otto Harrassowitz, 1954), 52, and Matthias Dall'Asta, "Bibliotheca trilinguis und 'dimidium animae': Johannes Reuchlin als Büchersammler," *Sammler und Bibliotheken im Wandel der Zeiten: Kongress in Hamburg am 20. und 21. Mai 2010*, ed. Sabine Graef, Sünje Prühlen and Walter Stork, *Zeitschrift für Bibliothekswesen und Bibliographie*, 100. Sonderband (Frankfurt am Main: Vittorio Klostermann, 2010), 117–43.

53. See Bloemendal, "In the Shadow of Donatus."

54. Enenkel, "Kommentare als multivalente Wissenssammlungen," 125.
55. On this commentary, see Maaike Zimmerman, "'Food for Thought' for Readers of Apuleius' *The Golden Ass*," in *Readers and Writers in the Ancient Novel*, ed. Michael Paschalis, Stelios Panayotakis and Gareth Schmelig. Ancient Narrative, Supplementum 12 (Groningen: Boekhuis and University Library, 2009), 218–40, esp. 219–21.
56. See Perrine Galand-Hallyn, "Les Miscellanées de Pietro Crinito: Une philologie de l'engagement et du lyrisme," *Ouvrages miscellanées et théorie de la connaissance à la Renaissance*, ed. Dominique de Courcelles (Paris: Publications de l'École nationale des chartes, 2003), 57–77.
57. On this work, see for instance Christoph Schönau, "Jacques Lefèvre d'Étaples, Quincuplex Psalterium (1509)," *Handbuch der Bibelhermeneutiken: Von Origenes bis zur Gegenwart*, ed. Oda Wischmeyer (Berlin: De Gruyter, 2016), 277–84.
58. See, e.g., Roberto Weiss, *The Dawn of Humanism in Italy* (New York: Haskell, 1947); Jozef IJsewijn, "The Coming of Humanism to the Low Countries," *Itinerarium Italicum: The Profile of the Italian Renaissance in the Mirror of its European Transformations: Dedicated to P.O. Kristeller on the Occasion of the 70th Birthday*, ed. Heiko Obermann and Thomas Brady Jr. (Leiden: Brill, 1974), 193–301.

Royal Netherlands Academy of Arts and Sciences, Huygens ING

jan.bloemendal@huygens.knaw.nl

Two Great Fable Authors from the Middle Ages—Marie de France and Ulrich Bonerius

New Perspectives on the Reception of an Ancient Literary Genre

ALBRECHT CLASSEN

Abstract

This study offers the first critical comparison between the fables composed by the Anglo-Norman Marie de France (late twelfth century) and by the Swiss-German Dominican priest Ulrich Bonerius (ca. 1350). Both poets drew heavily from classical sources, but both also injected personal comments and were quite creative each in his or her own ways. While there is no attempt here to argue that Marie might have influenced Bonerius, the comparison still allows us to recognize in many different ways how much both poets pursued parallel goals and were determined by similar ideals and values pertaining to the individual and human society. Especially Bonerius deserves greater attention and respect in medieval scholarship, as this comparative analysis illustrates quite dramatically. There are, of course, many similarities, but also significant differences between both poets, and yet they were undoubtedly masters in this genre of fables.

Our approach to medieval literature often depends on the specific filters and concepts used by researchers to evaluate, select, categorize, and qualify individual texts and poets, including or excluding them from the canon, which has always been highly problematic in the first place, even though often almost unavoidable considering the vast treasure trove of texts available from the Middle Ages or other periods.[1] This can have the curious consequence that an entire century might be more or less ignored, or that scholars focus only on one or two literary genres particularly developed at a certain period, and ignore many others. Of course, we also have to realize that the history of literature is filled with

Medievalia et Humanistica, New Series, Number 47 (Reinhold F. Glei and Maik Goth, eds.), Rowman & Littlefield, 2022.

an almost endless number of writers and poets, and it would be virtually impossible to do justice to them all. This automatically implies that our modern concerns and interests enter the picture, determining our selection of texts, for instance, whether they are "classical" or not. This has led to a dramatic transformation of our field of medieval studies over the last few decades, now also opening the perspective to such criteria as gender, race, colonialism, and power structures in the pre-modern world.[2]

The Case of Ulrich Bonerius

One striking example for this curious but unfortunately common disregard even of major writers or texts would be the fables by the Swiss-German Dominican priest Ulrich Bonerius contained in his *Edelstein* (The Gemstone) (ca. 1350), which represent a major steppingstone in the reception of ancient and early medieval models (Aesop, Babrius, Avianus, Anonymous Neveleti [Romulus], etc.) and which are yet hardly discussed in recent research.[3] Bonerius succeeds in offering extensive teachings about human failures, shortcomings, and vices, but also about the value of humility, intelligence, wisdom, and alacrity, and this in regularly entertaining and sharply formulated verse narratives. Specialized scholarship has certainly acknowledged his significant role in fourteenth-century literature, but in most cases his contemporaries who composed plays, mystical visions, and short verse narratives (*mæren*) occupy almost all of the scholarly attention.

This article intends to bring Bonerius back to the forefront of research on late medieval literature by way of analyzing a selection of his fables in direct comparison with those by his predecessor, Marie de France. By way of highlighting similarities and differences, Bonerius's unique literary qualities can be better assessed and evaluated. The former has already been fully recognized as a major poet of her time, both for her *lais* and her *fables*, so the latter also deserves the same respect and attention, but then as a major representative of fourteenth-century (Swiss-)German literature.

Bonerius's verse narratives, exactly one hundred of them, are framed by a prologue and an epilogue, a structural design that is the same model employed also in the contemporary *Decameron* by Boccaccio (also ca. 1350), a collection of prose tales, and also in the slightly earlier *Divina Commedia* by Dante Alighieri (completed ca. 1320). But Boccaccio did not necessarily offer specific teachings from an ethical or moral perspective, although we can still recognize behind each tale a concrete message about human behavior that would need to be corrected or improved. The storytellers primarily intend to entertain, but despite the laughter normally aroused,[4] there rest serious concerns about virtues and vices, human communication, love and sexuality, and social interactions. Bonerius is much more direct in his comments following each fable, which obviously strongly appealed to his contemporaries and posterity, considering that these fables have survived in thirty-six manuscripts and two early incunabula.[5]

History of Research on Bonerius

While Bonerius attracted greatest interest in the early history of German philology (late eighteenth and early nineteenth century, e.g., by Breitinger, Lessing, the Grimms, Beineke et al.), modern scholarship has not followed that lead and paid much less attention to him than he would certainly deserve, maybe because once it had become clear how much he drew from his ancient sources for his fables, the *Edelstein* did not seem to be particularly innovative as a work of literature *sui generis*.[6] This is rather unfortunate especially considering that the *Edelstein* easily proves to be, after all, a literary masterpiece both because of its new structural design in the history of medieval German fables and because of the poet's strong efforts to comment on the meaning of his fables in a more personal manner, offering concrete instructions and advice.[7]

Surprisingly, Bonerius does not even figure in major studies dealing with medieval German didactic literature, maybe because fables were not recognized as creative enough in that context.[8] However, for more than a hundred years during the late Middle Ages, Bonerius's fables enjoyed the status of being the best representatives of this genre; only by the late fifteenth century were they increasingly replaced by new collections, often pursuing different perspectives mirroring the rise of the Protestant Reformation.[9]

The History of Fables as a Genre

Fables cannot be viewed only through a narrow language-specific lens; instead, all of them belong to a global discourse on virtually the same concerns regarding human vices and virtues, behavior, morality, and ethics, commonly expressed by means of animal figures. Those animals talk and act in characteristic fashions, which then illuminate human behaviors; this in turn allows the listener/reader to learn from them and to improve him- or herself. This means, Bonerius's fables, as valuable as they certainly prove to be in terms of fourteenth-century German literature, really need to be studied in a wider context so that we can understand whether they were only translations or whether they represent innovative adaptations of sources after all. However, it would not be really helpful to examine the *Edelstein* in comparison with Indian, Persian, or Arabic sources, such as the famous collection *Kalila and Dimna, Marzubannama* by Marzuban (ca. 1220), or *Fakihat al-Khulafa' wa Mufakahat al-Zurafa'* by Ahmad ibn Arabshah (1389–1450), unless we search for archetypal motifs and themes on a global level.[10]

By contrast, and this will be the topic of this article, Bonerius continued the same literary tradition with his fables as the Anglo-Norman poet Marie de France did, whose *Fables* were some of the "bestsellers" of her time. She composed those shortly before 1200, so ca. 150 years before Bonerius set to work, and she also placed her fables, 103 in total, within the framework of a prologue and an epilogue. However, even though these two poets drew extensively on more or less the same Latin sources, both collections overlap only to some extent, and even in those cases where Bonerius worked with the same narrative plot in a specific fable, we still observe his very unique approach and personal contribution.

In order to better understand the fable as a major medieval literary genre within the European context, it seems most productive to read Marie's and Bonerius's collections side by side in order to gain a clear understanding of how they used the shared traditional material for their own specific purposes. I would not want to claim that the latter might have been influenced by the former, but if we consider Marie's *Fables* as literary masterpieces from the late twelfth century, which they certainly were according to the scholarly *opinio communis*,[11] then her Swiss-German successor in the middle of the fourteenth century also deserves to be placed right next to her.[12] An English translation of Bonerius's fables is now available, which makes the critical study even easier, especially for comparatists.[13]

Considering Marie's enormous popularity with her fables—they have survived in twenty-three manuscripts from the mid-thirteenth to the fifteenth century[14]—and keeping in mind that Bonerius's *Edelstein* has survived in thirty-six manuscripts from the late fourteenth to the sixteenth century (one burned in 1870), then we actually face two of the most important and influential vernacular fable authors of the entire Middle Ages writing in the vernacular. Reading the one without keeping the other in mind does a disservice to both and would blind us, once again, as if we still had to read medieval literature purely along linguistic divides. After all, both poets pursued very parallel strategies, relying heavily on a shared set of classical sources, but then both also incorporated other literary material, probably from a variety of oral sources, and then added their own creative inventions. The interesting question thus will be how Marie commented on her fables in contrast to and in comparison with Bonerius, who considerably expanded those sections of personal remarks in his fables and addressed his audience in very specific terms.

Marie de France and Ulrich Bonerius

As Harriet Spiegel emphasizes, "Marie did more than put these fables into verse; she made them her own. Most basically, she medievalizes her classical fables; hers are manifestly a product of the twelfth century, providing commentary on contemporary life, particularly on feudal social structure and questions of justice . . . and the people's awareness of what constitutes a beneficent kingship and their obligations of loyalty to a good ruler."[15] In comparison, German literary scholars from Georg Gottfried Gervinus (1805–1871) to Max Wehrli (1909–1998) have consistently praised Bonerius as a shining light in a rather dimly lit fourteenth century, as an intelligent, vivacious, realistic, and highly skilled poet.[16] Nevertheless, this poet hardly figures in recent research, which is not untypical of the situation concerning the long period between ca. 1300 and 1400.[17]

Intriguingly, both Marie and Bonerius work with numerous fables that are pretty much the same in each collection, and yet, which also proves to be most remarkable for both, each of them then added her or his own readings and thus transformed the respective fables into unique literary statements about social, political, moral, religious, philosophical, and ethical issues of relevance at the end of the twelfth and in the middle of the fourteenth century, and this in England and Switzerland respectively.

Both poets explain in prologues what the intentions of their collection of fables consist of, which are, not surprisingly, supposed to teach virtues and to convey inner happiness (Bonerius) or simply to provide knowledge (Marie) by way of negative examples. The Dominican author tends to go much more into detail and explains his motivations quite explicitly, stressing, for instance, that his fables serve to teach wisdom and intelligence, morality and ethics (66–70), whereas Marie proves to be more reticent and quickly goes straight to the core issues and leaves it up to the audience to figure out the inner meanings of her fables themselves.

She was quite content to refer simply to her anonymous patron, who wanted her to create this collection of fables, though she highly praises him as the flower of chivalry ("flurs est de chevalerie," 31), whereas Bonerius gives specific credit to his patron Johann von Ringgenberg (43–44), a wealthy and influential nobleman in the canton of Bern, known to us also for his courtly love poetry.[18] As Bonerius emphasizes most concretely, despite drawing from classical sources, he pursued his own ideals with these fables, through which the deeper meaning of life could be understood (69–76). He labeled his collection *Gemstone* because the true secrets of human existence are hidden and need to be explored by each individual, such as by way of reading these fables.[19]

Both poets set out with the famous account of the cock and the gemstone, in which the cock dismisses the valuable jewel because it cannot eat it, which means for both poets that the rooster was simply ignorant and could not understand the inner value of that gemstone. For Marie, this account serves her to criticize people who do not know how to prize the good and honorable and choose the worst instead of the best, proving to be bumbling in this life without having a clear sense of values and ideals (20–22). Bonerius goes much more into specifics and compares the rooster with those people who do not appreciate wisdom, the arts, honor, and their own property out of personal ignorance. For him, many individuals prove to be fools who do not have enough insight to embrace the true values in life that are hidden behind the material conditions.

Marie's fable no. 2, "The Wolf and the Lamb," appears only as no. 5 in Bonerius's work, but both address the same issue, with the wolf acting out the role of the mighty and powerful individuals who devour the weak and innocent out of greed and use an absurd explanation as justification for this murder, which we would call today nothing but "fake news." The wolf accuses the lamb/sheep of having soiled the water of the creek from which both are drinking, but the wolf stands upstream and the lamb/sheep downstream. Any disturbance of the water would hence be the result of the wolf's action. In both versions, the lamb/sheep tries to defend itself, pointing out its location and the wolf's erroneous claim, and also rejecting the charge that its own father had already insulted the wolf some time ago (in Marie: six months; in Bonerius: seven years). Marie has the lamb raise its voice rather meekly, though still in defiance. Bonerius develops the conversation between the sheep and the wolf

much further and gives the future victim considerably more assertive-
ness, insisting that it is not itself threatening in its own behavior, but the
other way around, the wolf assuming an aggressive posture (30), which
then results in murder.

Most importantly, Marie interprets her fable as a direct charge
against the nobles of her time ("Li vescunte e li jugeür," 32) who abuse
their power position to exploit the simple folks whom they force to
come to court, where they are falsely accused and then tried by corrupt
judges who make them to pay huge fines: "They strip them clean of
flesh and skin" (37). In Bonerius's case, the wolf represents those who
are guilty of arrogance (39) and deliberately cause injury to the poor
people. The poet bitterly condemns those who hold official authority and yet destroy the lives of their subjects out of an evil mind (46),
making children into orphans (48). He condemns these evil people
outright to suffering in hell in eternity (49) so that God's own glory
can shine forth. Marie argues only from a social and political perspective, warning about the threat of tyranny,[20] whereas Bonerius reveals
quite openly his ecclesiastic background and corresponding concerns.
Nevertheless, both poets share their strong criticism of corruption and
abuse of power among the administrators and governments, which
they equate with the rapacious wolf, whereas the innocent victims
among the people are represented by the lamb/sheep.

Differences between Marie de France and Ulrich Bonerius

Many times, however, despite strong plot similarities, the details can be
quite different. In "The Mouse and the Frog" (Marie: no. 3; Bonerius:
no. 6), the Anglo-Norman version begins with a pleasant scene where
the mouse has settled nicely into its new home at a mill and takes care
of itself. One day it is visited by a frog, whom the mouse invites in and
treats very generously. Both enjoy their companionship, which makes
the mouse believe that they can trust each other as friends. Thus, when
the frog in turn asks the mouse to come for a visit in its own home lo-
cated in a swamp, the latter trusts the frog completely and accompanies
it there, though they have to move through a meadow covered with dew.

Once having reached a river, the mouse, by then already being
completely wet, is about to despair, knowing only too well that it cannot swim and would drown. It does not realize the frog's murderous
strategy, and then even agrees to be tied to the frog's knee. As soon as
they are in the middle of the creek, the frog dives down in order to kill

the mouse (69). Frantically, the mouse struggles to survive, and all this commotion attracts a kite's attention, which swoops down, grabs both, and devours the fat frog, but it lets the meager mouse alone as it does not seem worthy as feed.

Bonerius takes us immediately into *media res*, with the frog and the mouse striking "eternal" friendship. The frog claims that it wants to help the mouse to return to its home, but in reality, it also pursues a murderous plan. The narrator emphasizes right away the frog's disloyalty (14) and the mouse's ignorance (16), which almost would have been the cause of the victim's drowning (20). The central issue here is that the frog breaks its promise of loyalty to the mouse: "sîn triuwe er an der miuse brach" (23), which results in the death of both because they are caught by a harrier and devoured one after the other. For the narrator, this serves as a valuable lesson not to trust those who speak differently than their deeds (37), and he warns the audience that those people would not gain much in honor who use deceptive words to hide their true intentions.

Moreover, Bonerius then underscores the grave danger for all people if they are challenged by someone who acts falsely and cheats. However, the narrator also points out that in the end, the frog also suffered its death, which means for him: "geschant al velscher müezin wesen!" (46; shamed/dishonored will be all those who are deceivers).

Marie changed her fable so that the villains here in life will never have real friends because they only know how to trick and deceive people. But there is at least some hope in her version because she entrusts that those evil individuals "place themselves in peril" (92). Despite these small differences in the plot, especially in the outcome, both poets embraced the same value condemning harshly all those who perform unethically and ultimately intend to get others killed through their devious plans, which is, unfortunately, a daily occurrence.

When we turn to "The City Mouse and the Country Mouse" (Marie: no. 9; Bonerius: no. 15), we notice the same degree of difference and similarity. In essence, the city mouse stays with the country mouse, and then invites the latter to come for a visit as well. The circumstances are not exactly the same, but in both narratives the two animals enjoy their simple but bountiful meal in peace and quiet. Next, we find both mice in the urban cellar where the city mouse has her luxurious dwelling with an endless amount of food available to her. But then they are disturbed, Marie referring to a butler, Bonerius to a cook, and both times the man comes down to the cellar, the city mouse quickly hides, knowing its way around very well, whereas its guest is terrified and lost in the unknown space, not aware of any escape route. Subsequently, once they are safe again, the country mouse decides to leave the city as fast as possible and to return home because in the woods it would be safe from people and their traps. For Marie, the lesson is simple and straightforward: "Each one prefers his small possession, / Which he enjoys in tranquil pleasure" (54–55). Not quite so Bonerius.

For him, the situation in the bountiful cellar represents the world itself, which deceives people through its external material attractions and hides the bitterness behind the physical illusion (50–51). The country mouse praises its own simple existence, despite its poverty (55), and projects an idyllic concept of its life free of danger and fear. Outside of the city, far away from all those dangers that come with the life in luxury, the individual would enjoy happiness (53 because "armuot ist âne sorge gar" (58; poverty is totally free of worries). Very much in the Boethian sense, the country mouse warns its companion that wealth always comes with many worries, whereas the poor person would be free from those. A life of poverty would not constitute any external dangers (63), whereas the rich people would constantly fear losing their wealth (64), not being able to find sound sleep (66). A life determined by fear would not be worth all the luxuries that one could receive temporarily (68–70), all of this clearly resonances of the fundamental teachings of the Catholic Church, but also those by Boethius in his *De consolatione philosophiae* (524).[21] By contrast, Marie only emphasizes that each person should be content with his or her lot ("le suen petit," 54) and should not try to compete with others who live under different circumstances.

In Marie's fable about the old lion (no. 14), the erstwhile mighty animal realizes that because of its old age, it has lost all of its power and now has become the butt of the joke of the other animals, which actually kick, stamp, and bite it out of disrespect.[22] The lion, helpless to defend itself any longer, thus offers the teaching that friends cannot be trusted if they offer their support only while the individual exerts much power or influence. Friendship thus easily proves to be nothing but a pretense in the world of the courts, as all those who had ever sworn their love will quickly disappear as soon as the other one has lost its strength and authority: "He has few friends who is not strong" (32).[23]

In Bonerius's version (no. 19), the very first message in the text addresses a very different observation concerning old age. While young people aspire for growing up quickly to gain a respectful position in society, those in power, hence those who are older, dislike being old due to the accompanying sicknesses and feebleness, meaning that no one is apparently happy with his or her actual age. Bonerius adds, reflecting on the realistic problems that all old people face at some point, that it proves to be highly valuable to have good friends even in old age, who would then take care of him or her (7–9).

Here, the old lion is badly abused by the various animals who all remember how much the lion used to hurt and insult them in the past. The lion realizes that its previous actions have now come around, to its detriment. In fact, the lion regrets, though it is too late for any repentance, its many evil deeds committed during its youth, which now, in its old age, it has to pay for badly. The fable concludes with the highly fitting proverb: It is a good thing to make friends, but it is better to keep them throughout one's life (36–37). Moreover, Bonerius goes one step further and warns his audience that all evil acts will eventually be punished (39–40), which undoubtedly mirrors, of course, a priest's perspective, but it also constitutes an innovative reading of the ancient Aesopian version.

The more we compare the fables by Marie and Bonerius, the more we realize the considerable differences between both poets, even though the core plot is commonly the same. In "The Swallow and the Linseed" (no. 17; Bonerius refers to "hemp," no. 23), for instance, the swallow realizes the great danger for them all if they do not combat the seeding of flax with which the farmer could make threads and ropes; and with these he could then create nets to catch the birds.

The bird's advice is to eat up those seeds and thus to destroy the harvest. The other swallows do not pay attention, and, even worse, fly back to their lord and share with him what the swallow had advised them to do. The latter, in return, goes to the farmer's land and builds its nest there, creating a kind of contract with him that allows it to be safe from any dangers coming from him. However, once the harvest has been brought in and threads have been produced, the farmer sets many traps and catches numerous other birds that had not been willing to listen to the swallow's advice. For Marie, the lesson is very clear; that is, the majority of people appear to be fools who do not want to listen to any advice and thus become victimized: "A fool who won't believe the wise" (30).

In Bonerius's version, the premise is the same, but the poet extrapolated the summit of the birds and gave the swallow much room to explain what it wants to advise the other birds to do. Those, however, ignore everything because the warning seems to be unnecessary ("ein spot," 27). Subsequently, the hemp grows well and is then harvested and transformed into ropes and nets, with which the other birds are then caught while seeking their food. In his epimythium, Bonerius raises the question of whether the one who does not want to accept good advice can avoid misfortune happening. Listening to and following good advice would result in good fortune (42). He also adds that those who are too trusting and feel too safe in their existence might lose their lives, although it would have been easy enough to avoid that danger early on.

The Topic of Freedom

Scholars have repeatedly noticed Bonerius's strong interest in the topic of freedom, as is expressed, for instance, in his fable no. 24: Of people who asked to get a king.[24] While Marie did not include this one, although it was also part of the fable collection by the Anonymous Neveleti (Romulus), the same theme comes through in the subsequent fable (Marie: no. 18), which is also present in Bonerius's collection, no. 25: "Of Frogs That Wanted to Have a King."

But let us look at Marie's version first. Here, the frogs want to improve their lot, although they had enjoyed freedom for generations and have no apparent reason to complain. Instead of being content with their pond, they want to move to the firm land, for which they need, as they think, a king ("A la tere vodreient aler," 6; "And wished to move to solid ground"). Destiny then fulfills that wish, throwing a log into their pond, the true nature of which the frogs recognize quickly, sitting on it and covering it with their feces, so much so that it sinks to the bottom. Upon their repeated appeals, Destiny then sends an adder as their king, which immediately begins to devour the frogs as food. When the remaining frogs complain again, Destiny refuses to listen to them any further, blaming them badly for having "shamed churlishly that seignior" (43).

The poet uses this fable as an occasion to criticize those people who belittle and demean their own lord and do not respect him. Instead of demonstrating their good citizenship, they disregard their king and then reap the negative profit of being subjugated by an evil lord under whom they cannot even survive. Marie does not criticize at all kingship in itself, but she also acknowledges that there could be bad and good kings. Further, in her perspective, there is a symbiotic relationship between the king and the people, neither one being able to exist without the other: "They always want to stamp their lord; / His honour they don't know to guard" (47–48). Indirectly, under the cover of the fable, she thus contributed to the ongoing discourse about the good ruler, which was normally described in texts called "Mirror for Princes."[25]

Bonerius develops this fable by including many small but significant details that are different from those in Marie's narrative. The frogs enjoy both their aquatic and terrestrial world and are completely free, being in no need of a ruler or a king (5–6). The one verse that Bonerius injects here deserves particular attention because it represents a rather unusual comment for a medieval poet, strongly advocating freedom in every respect: "in vrîheit stuont ir aller muot" (7; they all wanted to have their freedom). But the frogs are not happy with their status because they cannot stand this freedom and want to be gloriously represented by a king. Not Destiny, but Jupiter finally feels obliged to consent to their requests and throws a log into the pond. He has to laugh about the foolish frogs (14), indicating thereby how little he respects their demand, which is, at least in his mind, a stupidity. As so often in medieval literature, this laughter exposes a significant realization and initiates an important change of events.[26]

After the frogs have regained their courage and have sat irreverently on the log, their laments reach a new level, all of them complaining bitterly but foolishly that they could not live in a decent manner without a king: "der wol richten möcht ir leben" (32; who could govern their lives well). Tired of the frogs' constant chatter, Jupiter then sends a stork, which even more greedily than the adder attacks and kills the frogs, who only then realize the danger they have put themselves into. But Jupiter subsequently no longer listens to the frogs' renewed laments and lets the stork rule in the way it wants and tells the frogs that they have deserved their own destiny (51).

Bonerius's epimythium offers a number of noteworthy comments about freedom, slavery, and independence. He emphasizes that the person who can be his or her own lord should not aspire to become a servant (32). Beyond this political statement, however, the poet then also turns to ethical and moral issues, stressing that the one who owns enough for his or her living should be content with it and not ask for more (33–34). A person who wants to preserve the own inner peace and happiness ought not to submit to a lord, if there is no need or force to do so (58–59). Bonerius does not conclude with a final political observation but turns the fable around and argues that people ought to accept what they have and be happy with it: "so im wol sî, daz hab verguot" (60; if you are content, then regard this as good). Lusting after more than what an individual might need could easily turn into great misfortune (61–62).

For Marie, this fable provided a good platform to reflect on reasonable political conditions within the monarchical system, whereas for Bonerius it served first to idealize the value of freedom, particularly in a political context, and then to warn against a lack of self-contentment, also in an ethical, material, and moral sense: "wil er ruowe und êr behân" (57; if he or she wants to have inner peace and honor). While

Marie addresses primarily public concerns that pertain to the entire society, Bonerius is more interested in the individual's decision regarding his or her relationship with society at large.

In the fable "The Thief and the Dog" (Marie: no. 20; Bonerius: no. 27), a thief tries to bribe a dog not to bark and to let him steal at night. The dog flatly refuses the bribe and the temptation to betray its own master, the shepherd. The fundamental danger of treason thus finds its vivid expression here, a topic of considerable interest and concern throughout the entire Middle Ages, as many legal, literary, religious, and political documents confirm.[27] Both poets focus explicitly on the severe crime of treason and warn their audiences to abstain from a short-term gain (bribe), which would take away one's lifelong support and supply. Marie strongly praises the dog for its strong character, which enables it to resist the thief's flattery and false promise. Her fable expresses this message in a spiffy and concise manner, leaving no doubt as to the specific warning about treason as one of the worst offenses in a feudal relationship.

Bonerius follows suit, but he expands the conversation between dog and thief considerably. The dog explicitly points out that the bread offered by the thief actually contains poison, or gall (17), which would rob it of all of its future food supplied by its master. Rejecting the thief's offer, the dog ensures that its entire life with its own master will be secure; the food offered one night by the thief would never be equal to its regular food supply provided to it in return for its service guarding the herds. In other words, it would barter lifelong security for a one-night allure.

This then allows the poet to ruminate further on the nature of gifts that always obligate the receiver to the giver. Hence, it would be extremely important to consider carefully who is offering the gift and what it would imply, especially if it might hide an evil intention (38). Only if one were to understand fully the motivation of the gift giver would the gift be worth receiving—a significant observation already made by the anonymous poet of the Old English *Beowulf* (ca. 700; Unferth's sword Hrunting) and by the equally anonymous poet of the Old High German "Hildebrandslied" (ca. 820; Hildebrand's gold rings) and that proved to be a critical issue in many subsequent texts throughout the entire Middle Ages and beyond, such as in the many courtly romances.[28]

Both Marie and Bonerius obviously chose this tale from the ancient fable tradition because it addressed so effectively some of the central issues in medieval society, such as treason, as we find it also treated by Dante in his *Inferno* (*Divina Commedia*, completed in ca. 1320), represented by the ominous Count Ugolino della Gherardesca, who is "imprisoned" in the ice of the second ring (Antenora) of the lowest circle.[29] Marie appears to be more concerned with the political implications, warning her audience also about the danger of flattery (32), whereas Bonerius focuses more on the general relationship among people and the ethical issue of gift-giving.

In "The Wolf and the Dog" (Marie: no. 26; Bonerius: no. 59), the issue of freedom emerges again, this time explored in the conversation between these two animals. The wolf is greatly impressed by the dog's fine appearance, being well fed and healthy, and it would like to receive the same good treatment from the dog's master. But then, the wolf also discovers, in Marie's version, that the dog is wearing a collar and is dragging a chain, both attributes, so to speak, of its servitude and dependence on the human owner. If he were not tied up during the day, as the dog explains, he would be uncontrolled and might chew on all kinds of objects in his master's possession and destroy them. At night, however, his job is to guard the entire farm.

For the wolf, this amounts to a form of slavery, and it is absolutely abhorred by this dangerous condition, which it might run into only because of its desire to be well fed on a regular basis. So, it announces immediately: "'. . . I'll never choose to wear a chain! / I'd rather live as a wolf, free, / Than on a chain in luxury. / I still can make a choice, and so / You fare to town; to woods I'll go.'" (36–40). More we are not told, except that subsequently the friendship between the wolf and the dog is terminated. Curiously, this would then explain the global hostility among both types of animals, but in essence, as this fable indicates, the wolf really emerges as the hero because it knows how to appreciate freedom, whereas the dog displays a servile attitude. Many other times, the fables cast the wolf as a dangerous, untrustworthy animal, but here it emerges as a true hero, a champion of personal independence already in the modern sense of the word.

Bonerius more or less pursues the same agenda, varying only in small details, such as that the wolf notices, not a collar or a leash, but the dog's scratched and shaved neck, which is, as the dog explains, the result of wearing the collar. The wolf, once having understood the situation of the dog, promulgates its absolute dedication to freedom, which it would never abandon in favor of food. More explicitly than Marie, Bonerius outlines the wolf's fundamental value concerning freedom, emphasizing that a poor man would be richer than the wealthy one if he could maintain his free will, whereas the other would have to carry out service, like a slave (63–67). All the material objects in this world would not balance out the value of the free will that adds honor to all deeds and words (71–76). The one who would have to give up this free will would be a miserable person, irrespective of all of his or her money or property: "vrîheit gât vûr allez guot / der welte, wer sîn vrîgen muot / ûf gît umb silber und umb golt, / dem wirt ze teil des riuwen solt" (79–82; Freedom supersedes all goods in the world, and she or he who abandons the free spirit in return for silver and gold will at the end regret it). The similarity of this version to the one by Marie is significant, but the Swiss poet emphasized the value of freedom considerably more strongly than his predecessor.[30]

Ethics in Everyday Life

The short fable "The Cricket and the Ant" (Marie: no. 39; Bonerius: no. 42) offers valuable insights into fundamental work ethics represented by these two insects.[31] While it is a cricket in Marie's text, Bonerius refers to the locust, but this has no bearing on the critical issues here.[32]

In the Anglo-Norman version, the cricket crawls upon an anthill during wintertime on its desperate search for food. Upon the ant's inquiry as to what it had done during the summer, the cricket relates that it had always entertained people with its singing, but it did not collect food, as the ant busily had done the entire time. The ant then refuses to help the cricket because it would not be able to return any aid and should have taken care of itself when the time was right (25–26).

Bonerius's version proves to be much more detailed (68 verses in contrast to 28 verses in Marie's text) and offers a full narrative that leads to an extensive discussion of social conditions. He begins immediately with a proverb expressing that precaution proves to be a good protection against future dangers (1–2), which he applies to human life, from youth to old age. The ant, as we are told, works hard from early summer until the onset of winter and thus has enough provisions when it needs them urgently. We are told in detail how it struggles hard all day from early in the morning until late in the evening (19–21), getting little sleep. As soon as the first frost arrives, all the ants withdraw into their well-stocked ant pile (26–28).

The locust then begs the ant for food because it is really afraid of dying from famine (32), since frost and snow cover the ground, i.e., a reference to winter, which proves to be a rather rare phenomenon in medieval literature.[33] During the summer, as we are then told, the locust had mocked the ant for its busyness, whereas now it is in desperate need of help, which the ant, however, denies, obviously out of a sense of strong irritation. While the ant had made the greatest efforts all the time to secure its food, the locust did nothing but jump around, carelessly enjoying its free time (49–51).

From this concrete situation involving the two insects, the poet then extrapolates and offers a global message about how young people ought to prepare themselves for their adult life and also old age. Only those who, in their youth, would aim for achieving esteem and capabilities would later also experience a good life. Bonerius then concludes with yet another proverb, concerning the necessity to smite the iron while it is still hot, and applies this to human life at large: "die wil der junge krefte hât, / sô werb um guot, daz ist mîn rât" (67–68; while the young person has strength she or he ought to acquire goods, that is my advice). This Dominican priest once again demonstrates his primary concern regarding a good, virtuous life, which can be achieved if one takes the right precaution, works hard in one's youth, and prepares well for later years.

Alternative Narratives Within the Fable Context

Not all the verse narratives in Marie's *Fables* and in Bonerius's *Edelstein* are actually "fables," with animals, birds, or insects as the acting figures. Significantly, both poets also resorted to the well-known account of the "Widow of Ephesus," first recorded in the *Satyricon* by Petronius (first century CE), and elaborated it each in their own ways.[34] To summarize Marie's approach (no. 25), we first hear of a man's death and his widow's great grief, mourning him day and night, spending all her time right next to his grave. Concurrently, a thief is hanged nearby, that is, outside of the cemetery. A knight, who is the thief's relative, cuts down the corpse and buries it to avoid public shame to fall upon his family, although this had been strictly forbidden on the threat of death. Deeply worried about the consequences of his deed, he approaches the widow and pleads with her to help him in this situation. It is unclear what the verse "Dit li que ele se cunfortast" (21) might really imply, whether sexual pleasures or consolation for her husband's death in general (maybe his offer to marry her). At any rate, she quickly offers him her husband's corpse because, as she comments, "One ought to use the dead to free / The living, who can comfort be" (35–36).

This concludes the fable, and the poet only remarks in her epimythium that the dead cannot trust the living to take good care of them, which then leads to the global lament: "Tant est li mund faus e jolis" (40; The world's so false and frivolous). Marie does not address the widow's action any further, and we also do not learn anything about the knight and his relationship with the woman, which ensures that the narrative does not assume any particularly misogynist tone of voice.

In Bonerius's tale (no. 57), the situation proves to be much more complex and actually hostile to women, even though the poet later tries hard, at least in the subsequent fable (no. 58) and elsewhere, to depict women in a very different light, then even giving much praise to worthy and protective mothers (no. 33) and to powerful and strong noble ladies (no. 96). Here, at first, the widow displays sincere grief and sorrow, lamenting and crying for days and nights right next to the grave. Neither rain nor snow can drive her away because her ardent love for her deceased husband fills her heart (18–19).

During that time, a man is hanged at the gallows, and an official is placed near him so that the thief's relatives cannot remove the dead man secretly and bury him. The official knows very well that the judge would have him decapitated if he were derelict in his duties, especially, as the subsequent events immediately bring to light, because the family members of the hanged man obviously feel deeply shamed by the public exhibition of the body and are most anxious to untie him from the gallows and bury him. Hardly has the official left his post, attracted by the fire that the widow keeps going, when someone from that family moves in and cuts down the body. We are not told anything about the details and only learn that the corpse has disappeared once the guard returns to the gallows. Historical records confirm many times that such situations actually occurred more often than not and that the authorities faced a serious problem after they had a convicted person hanged.[35]

Not only does the guard neglect his duties, but he is also immediately attracted to the widow and begs her to sleep with him, which she happily agrees with, quickly forgetting all of her previous sorrow and her love for her dead husband. The narrator thus characterizes both in a very negative light, and their subsequent action, digging up the corpse of her dead husband and hanging it at the gallows as a replacement for the thief, adds another level of egregious moral and ethical transgression. The guard promises her that she will be able to overcome all of her sorrows and to support her body and soul to regain happiness (53–56), and both then engage in a sexual act, which the narrator describes in curiously endearing terms: "gar lieplîch er si umbe vieng, / vil liebes er mit ir begieng" (65–66; most lovingly he embraced her; he did something very erotic with her).

Afterward, the official returns to his post but realizes to his horror that the corpse has been removed, a precarious situation which now endangers his own life. Not knowing what to do, he goes back to the woman and relates to her what has happened. Indeed, she immediately offers him her own dead husband as a replacement, and both then go to work to dig out the corpse and to hang it at the gallows.

For Bonerius, this illustrates particularly the danger coming from immoral and untrustworthy women at large. In fact, he warns his audience that much misfortune will be done by evil women (104–5), a situation for which humankind has already had to pay dearly (106), as illustrated by the so-called victimization of classical victims such as Adam, Paris, Sampson, and Solomon (107–10).[36] The same trope also appears in the near-contemporary Middle English alliterative romance, *Sir Gawain and the Green Knight* (ca. 1370) and in many other contexts.[37]

The poet drew, just like Marie, from a classical source (Petronius), but he places most of the blame on the widow and nearly ignores the action (seduction) by the guard, and this despite the fact that he was responsible for his own dire situation. However, Bonerius discriminates further, at least to some extent, and only criticizes "boese[ ] wîben" (101; evil women), which makes sense in light of the next fable, where we hear of three widows who adamantly refuse to marry again and insist on observing their honor, chastity, and inner character instead of looking for another husband. Nevertheless, the misogyny in no. 57 is very obvious, though not unexpected for medieval narratives composed by a male poet. But we still can acknowledge Bonerius's considerable skill in dramatizing the exchange, with elaborate dialogues and skillful handling of the figures' movements, giving the widow, despite her being negatively evaluated at the end, considerable agency determining her life.

Strategy and Methodology

Finally, let us compare the last fable in both collections before the epilogue to gain a better sense of the individual approaches pursued by both poets. Marie relates, in fable no. 103, the exchange between a woman and her hen, which is scratching all day in search of worms. Although the woman offers to feed the hen regularly with grain, the hen rejects this offer because it would never abandon its own nature, that is, this constant search for worms in the earth. For the poet, this means that people can never change their character or mindset, even if they possess great wealth and would not need to strive any longer for an income. In sum, Marie argues, which is in a way the crowning conclusion from all of her fables, that people never improve their nature: "Tuz jurs coveitent en lur curage" (26; "[they cannot change] the lust within, for all their days"). The epilogue, however, then does not engage with any of the ideas previously formulated in the fables.

The last "fable" in Bonerius's *Edelstein* might actually be the best of the entire collection, and it systematically leads to the epilogue. In no. 100, "Of a King and a Barber," we are confronted with two separate but interlinked settings. First, a highly learned priest—maybe an allusion to the poet himself?—attends a market where he sells "grôz wîsheit" (16; great wisdom), such as all of these fables. The king learns about this unusual "merchant" and sends his servants to buy some of that "commodity." Although the priest charges a large amount, which the servants regard as a ridiculously high price (40), he offers nothing but one written statement in Latin, but here translated into German for the current context: "du solt daz end an sehen / dînr werken, und waz dir beschehen / mag dar umbe künfteklîch" (35–37; keep the end of your deeds in mind and think what might happen to you as a consequence).

Although the servants grumble about this "poor" deal, the king is happy with the advice and has it inscribed above the door to his room in golden letters. Soon afterward, a group of courtiers intends to have the king assassinated, and they bribe the barber to carry out the murder on their behalf. However, as soon as the barber has read those words, he trembles badly, and his face becomes deathly pale, which awakens the king's suspicion; he has the barber apprehended, who then confesses what his intention had been. Thus, the king preserved his own life, while the disloyal courtiers had to escape (85–87).

Bonerius's epimythium offers the important lesson that the person who keeps his or her own death in mind would be wise because there would not be any regret about a wasted or wrong life at the moment of death. This then allows the poet to conclude: "guot ende guoten namen gît" (94; a good ending grants a good name [honor]). Keeping one's mortality in mind would transform one's own life entirely: "wer sich in daz ende leit, / der gewinnet selten leit" (101–2; the person who embraces the own end will rarely suffer from sorrow). Of course, Bonerius does not only mean death itself but, rather, the human soul and its afterlife. This then also finds its confirmation in the epilogue, where the poet emphasizes the importance of reading fables carefully and focusing on the conclusion in order to discover the truth behind the narrative, which directly connects with the very first fable about the gemstone and the need to read its inner meaning in order to reveal its true value.

Wisdom

The purpose of the genre of fables thus consists of gaining wisdom: "dar umb list man ein bîschaft guot, / daz wîser werd des menschen muot" (7–8; we read a good fable so that we gain true wisdom). Bonerius admits that his poetic skills are not well developed, but he hopes that his audience would understand, if they comprehend the next metaphor, that great sweetness can rest behind a simple peal. Or a small or unimportant garden might produce just the right fruit that could provide solace for people's suffering (15–18). Moreover, Bonerius also underscores that those in need of advice and consolation would not profit from sophisticated words if the advice would be useless (23–24). However, there are, as he also observes, many highfaluting preachers who do not even understand their own words (25–26), whereas he hopes that his straightforward fables will achieve the desired effect of providing teaching to his audience. His fables serve, as he underscores, to help people gain happiness in their lives and to protect them from the horrible suffering in the infernal afterlife.

Marie, by contrast, in her epilogue, limits her remarks mostly to her efforts in translating these fables from Anglo-Saxon to Anglo-Norman (12), referring to King Alfred, who had allegedly translated the Aesopian fables into "engleis" (17), whereas she rendered them into "franceis" (18). Scholarship has been able to trace only the first forty of Marie's fables to a specific source, the Romulus, or Anonymous Neveleti, whereas the remaining sixty-three could not be identified more specifically regarding their source—unless those were her own creations.[38] In the case of Bonerius, we know more details about where he drew his inspirations from, and yet there as well the poet added much of his own comments and lessons, which consistently criticized or ridiculed foolish people.

Both poets primarily targeted, with their fables, foolish, ignorant, stupid, greedy, or disloyal people, such as the ignorant knight in Marie's fable no. 101 who does not know where to travel and gets only absurd advice from a wise old man who thus exposes the ridiculous nature of this question. Bonerius offers his own satirical comments in fable no. 99, ridiculing a knight's stupid son who, despite a costly education in Paris, never learns anything and proves, upon his return, that even the best teachers cannot transform a boorish and ignorant person into an intelligent and educated individual.

To be sure, this is the essential purpose of all fable literature across the world, and the works by the Anglo-Norman and the Swiss-German poet do not differ from it in that regard. Despite, or rather because of, at times rather strong differences in the plots of these two fable authors, they confirm the extent to which both Marie de France and Ulrich Bonerius can be counted among the best poets of fables in the twelfth and the fourteenth centuries. Both strongly targeted the shortcomings and failures of people in their respective societies and effectively utilized the ancient tradition launched by Aesop for their own purposes.

Tragically, or ironically, in light of their verse narratives, we might have to conclude that the roles of vices and virtues in human life have not changed much at all. While Marie often proves to be rather curt and direct, almost to the point where her social criticism of the evil lords might become dangerous for herself, Bonerius develops his fables significantly and transforms them into lively narratives with great entertainment and didactic effect. Yet, however we view the *Fables* and the *Edelstein*, both demonstrated the great importance of this genre, which each poet understood exceedingly well how to develop and to present to their respective audiences.

To draw from one more example, in fable no. 7, "The Wolf and the Crane," Marie outlines the rapacious behavior of the mighty aristocrats of her time and laments that they badly abuse their subjects without granting them any reward for their labor. This finds its parallel in Bonerius's fable no. 11, "Of a Wolf and a Crow," where the wolf, having been saved by the crow from suffocating, does not repay the service and only points out that it had let the crow live while it grabbed with its beak the bone out of the wolf's throat.

Marie targets evil lords and chastises them badly for their viciousness, whereas Bonerius pursues a more differentiating approach, advising his audience to provide service only to good people, who actually pay, and to stay away from the evil ones, who do not pay. Marie directly aimed at the mean-spirited members of her own social class, the aristocracy, whereas Bonerius warned more generally about untrustworthy people at large ("dem argen") who are determined by an evil mind ("swacher muot," 58). Irrespective of the differences, large and small, between the fables told by Marie and those by Bonerius, both poets successfully formulated timeless messages about right and wrong behavior and thereby created a literary portrait of basic faults and shortcomings among all people of their time. Those messages continue to speak to us today rather deeply, so both poets deserve great respect for their accomplishments, and this also by modern readers.

Notes

1. While the contributors to *Vergessene Texte des Mittelalters*, ed. Nathanael Busch and Björn Reich (Stuttgart: S. Hirzel, 2014) try hard to open the gates to the vast literary archives, the contributors to *Klassiker des Mittelalters*, ed. Regina Toepfer. Spolia Berolinensia, 38 (Hildesheim: Weidmannsche Verlagsbuch-handlung, 2019), return to the very same old canon of Middle High German literature; cf. also Albrecht Classen, "The Torturous and Random Process of the Canonization in Literary History from the Middle Ages to the Present. The Case of Erasmus Widmann as an Example—The Victimization of a Poet Oddly Situated between Epochs, Cultures, and Religions," *Studia Neophilologica* 83, no. 1 (2011): 94–103.

2. Ken Mondschein, "Liberal Arts for Social Change," *Humanities*, online (forthcoming). See the bibliography relevant for these new approaches by Jonathan Hsy and Julie Orlemanski, "Race and Medieval Studies: A Partial Bibliography," *Postmedieval: A Journal of Medieval Cultural Studies* 8 (2017): 500–31; and now Geraldine Heng, *The Invention of Race in the European Middle Ages* (New York and Cambridge: Cambridge University Press, 2018). Cf. already Lisa Lampert, "Race, Periodicity, and the (Neo-) Middle Ages," *Modern Language Quarterly* 65, no. 3 (2004): 391–421.

3. The text-image relationship in many of the Bonerius manuscripts represents an interesting exception to the sidelining of this poet; see, for instance, Kattrin Schlecht, *Fabula in Situ: Äsopische Fabelstoffe in Text, Bild und Gespräch*. Scrinium Friburgense, 37 (Berlin and Boston: Walter de Gruyter, 2014); René Wetzel, "Diebold Laubers ysopus gemolt? Zur Boner-Handschrift Cod. Bodmer 42 (G) in der Bibliotheca Bodmeriana, Cologny-Genf," in *Aus der Werkstatt Diebold Laubers*, ed. Christoph Fasbender, Claudia Kanz, and Christoph Winterer. Kulturtopographie des Alemannischen Raums 3 (Berlin and Boston: Walter de Gruyter, 2012), 257–85.

4. *Laughter in the Middle Ages and Early Modern Times: Epistemology of a Fundamental Human Behavior, Its Meaning, and Consequences*, ed. Albrecht Classen. Fundamentals of Medieval and Early Modern Culture, 5 (Berlin and New York: Walter de Gruyter, 2010).

5. Walter Mitzka, "Boner, Ulrich," *Neue Deutsche Biographie*, ed. Otto zu Stolberg-Wernigerode, (Berlin: Duncker & Humblot, 1955), 2:443; online at: https://www.deutsche-biographie.de/pnd118661418.html#ndbcontent.; Klaus Grubmüller, "Boner," in *Die deutsche Literatur des Mittelalters: Verfasserlexikon*, 2nd ed., completely revised, ed. Kurt Ruh et al. (Berlin and New York: Walter de Gruyter, 1978), vol. 1, cols. 947–52; Ulrich Boner, *Der Edelstein: Eine mittelalterliche Fabelsammlung*. Zweisprachige Ausgabe Mittelhochdeutsch—Neuhochdeutsch. Herausgegeben, übersetzt, mit Anmerkungen, farbigen Abbildungen, einem Nachwort, Literaturverzeichnis, Register und Fabel-Verzeichnis versehen von Manfred Stange (Uberstadt-Weiher, Heidelberg, and Neustadt a. d. W., and Basel: verlag regionalkultur, 2016).

6. Klaus Grubmüller, *Meister Esopus: Untersuchungen zur Geschichte und Funktion der Fabel im Mittelalter*. Münchener Texte und Untersuchungen zur deutschen Literatur des Mittelalters, 56 (Zürich and Munich: Artemis, 1977); Adalbert Elschenbroich, *Die deutsche und lateinische Fabel in der Frühen Neuzeit*, 2 vols. (Tübingen: Max Niemeyer, 1990). Klaus Grubmüller, *Meister Esopus: Untersuchungen zur Geschichte und Funktion der Fabel im Mittelalter*. Münchener Texte und Untersuchungen zur deutschen Literatur des Mittelalters, 56 (Zürich

and Munich: Artemis, 1977); Aaron E. Wright, *"Hie lert uns der meister." Latin Commentary and the German Fable 1350–?1500.* Medieval and Renaissance Texts and Studies, 218 (Tempe, AZ: Arizona Center for Medieval and Renaissance Studies, 2001), 107–31.

7. Björn Reich and Christoph Schanze, "'Wer die bîschaft merken wil, der setz sich ûf des endes zil': einführende Überlegungen zum Verhältnis von 'narratio' und 'moralisatio,'" *Beiträge zur mediävistischen Erzählforschung* 1 (2018): 101–22, draw on Bonerius's didactic explanations in the epilogue to illustrate what the entire volume of this journal aims to achieve, but they do not offer a fully-fledged reading of any of his fables. None of the contributors to *Dichtung und Didaxe: Lehrhaftes Sprechen in der deutschen Literatur des Mittelalters,* ed. Henrike Lähnemann and Sandra Linden (Berlin and New York: Walter de Gruyter, 2009) even considers Bonerius, and the genre of fables is also hardly mentioned.

8. Bruno Boesch, *Lehrhafte Literatur: Lehre in der Dichtung und Lehrdichtung im deutschen Mittelalter.* Grundlagen der Germanistik, 21 (Berlin: Erich Schmidt Verlag, 1977), barely mentions the fable, and entirely ignores Bonerius (226–27).

9. For a very compact and detailed outline of the history of the fable, see the entry in *Metzler Literatur Lexikon: Begriffe und Definitionen,* ed. Günther and Irmgard Schweikle, 2nd rev. ed. (Stuttgart: J. B. Metzler, 1990), 147–48; Harold J. Blackham, *The Fable as Literature* (London and Dover, NH: Athlone Press 1965); Gerd Dicke and Klaus Grubmüller, *Die Fabeln des Mittelalters und der frühen Neuzeit: ein Katalog der deutschen Versionen und ihrer lateinischen Entsprechungen.* Münstersche Mittelalter-Schriften, 60 (Munich: Wilhelm Fink, 1987); Reinhard Dithmar, *Die Fabel: Geschichte, Struktur, Didaktik.* 8th rev. ed. Rpt. of the completely rev. ed. from 1988. Uni-Taschenbücher, 73 (1988; Paderborn and Munich: Schöningh, 1997); David Lee Rubin and A. L. Sells, "Fable," *The New Princeton Encyclopedia of Poetry and Poetics,* ed. Alex Preminger and T. V. F. Brogan (Princeton, NJ: Princeton University Press, 1993), 400–401; Hans Georg Coenen, *Die Gattung Fabel: Infrastrukturen einer Kommunikationsform.* Uni-Taschenbücher, 2159 (Göttingen: Vandenhoeck & Ruprecht, 2000).

10. Munshi, Nasrullah, *Kalila and Dimna,* trans. from the Persian by Wheeler Thackston (Indianapolis, IN, and Cambridge: Hackett Publishing, 2019).

11. See the various contributions to Marie's *fables* in *A Companion to Marie de France,* ed. Logan E. Whalen. Brill's Companions to the Christian Tradition, 27 (Leiden and Boston: Brill, 2011), such as by Emanuel J. Mickel Jr, Matilda Tomaryn Bruckner, and Charles Brucker.

12. Marie de France, *Fables,* ed. and trans. Harriet Spiegel, Medieval Academy Reprints for Teaching (Toronto, Buffalo, and London: University of Toronto Press, 1994). For an extensive discussion of her *fables* in aesthetic and semiological terms, see R. Howard Bloch, *The Anonymous Marie de France* (Chicago and London: University of Chicago Press, 2003), 111–97. See also Sharon Kinoshita and Peggy McCracken, *Marie de France: A Critical Companion.* Gallica, 24 (Woodbridge, Suffolk: Boydell & Brewer, 2012), 91–104, who read her *fables* mostly in terms of the poet's critical evaluation of feudalism and the abuse of power at the royal court.

13. *The Fables of Ulrich Bonerius (ca. 1350): Masterwork of Late Medieval Didactic Literature,* trans. Albrecht Classen (Newcastle-upon Tyne: Cambridge Scholars Publishing, 2020).

14. Marie de France, *Fables*, ed. and trans. Spiegel (see note 12); cf. also http://www.utm.edu/staff/bobp/vlibrary/mdfrancemss.shtml (last accessed on Aug. 18, 2020).
15. Marie de France, *Fables*, ed. and trans. Spiegel (see note 12), 9–10.
16. For a brief summary, see Ulrich Boner, *Der Edelstein*, ed. and trans. Stange (see note 5), 426.
17. Johannes Janota, *Orientierung durch volkssprachige Schriftlichkeit (1280/90–1380/90)*. Geschichte der deutschen Literatur von den Anfängen bis zum Beginn der Neuzeit, III: Vom späten Mittelalter zum Beginn der Neuzeit (Tübingen: Max Niemeyer, 2004), 300–303. He praises Bonerius, but his comments are barely more than a footnote. Reich and Schanze, "'Wer die bîschaft merken wil" (see note 7), only discuss Bonerius's didactic strategy at large.
18. *Der Minnesänger von Ringgenberg. Ein illustrierter Beitrag über den Minnesänger Johannes von Ringgenberg*, ed. Eduard Buri and Rudolf Gallati (Interlaken: Schlaefli, 1984); see also https://de.wikipedia.org/wiki/Johann_von_Ringgenberg (last accessed on Aug. 20, 2020).
19. Reich and Schanze, "'Wer die bîschaft merken wil" (see note 7), emphasize this point above all, but do not go into further details regarding Bonerius's texts.
20. Albrecht Classen, "The People Rise Up against the Tyrants in the Courtly World: John of Salisbury's *Policraticus*, the *Fables* by Marie de France and the Anonymous *Mai und Beaflor*," *Neohelicon* 35, no. 1 (2008): 17–29.
21. Boethius, *Consolation of Philosophy*, trans., with intro. and notes, by Joel C. Relihan (Indianapolis, IN, and Cambridge: Hackett Publishing, 2001), prose five in book II; for critical comments, see *Boethius in the Middle Ages: Latin and Vernacular Traditions of the "Consolatio philosophiae,"* ed. Maarten J. F. M. Hoenen and Lodi Nauta. Studien und Texte zur Geistesgeschichte des Mittelalters, 58 (Leiden: Brill, 1997); *Vernacular Traditions of Boethius's De Consolatione philosophiae*, ed. Noel Harold Kaylor, Jr. and Philip Edward Phillips. Research in Medieval Culture (Kalamazoo, MI: Medieval Institute Publications, Western Michigan University, 2016); *Remaking Boethius: The English Language Translation Tradition of The Consolation of Philosophy*, ed. Brian Donaghey, Noel Harold Kaylorm, Philip Edward Phillips, and Paul E. Szarmach. Arizona Studies in the Middle Ages and Renaissance, 40 (Tempe, AZ: Arizona Center for Medieval & Renaissance Studies, 2019).
22. For many approaches to old age in the pre-modern world, see the contributions to *Old Age in the Middle Ages and the Renaissance: Interdisciplinary Approaches to a Neglected Topic*, ed. Albrecht Classen. Fundamentals of Medieval and Early Modern Culture, 2 (Berlin and New York: Walter de Gruyter, 2007).
23. *Friendship in the Middle Ages and Early Modern Age: Explorations of a Fundamental Ethical Discourse*, ed. Albrecht Classen and Marilyn Sandidge. Fundamentals of Medieval and Early Modern Culture, 6 (Berlin and New York: Walter de Gruyter, 2010).
24. Ulrich Boner, *Der Edelstein*, ed. and trans. Stange (see note 5), 422–23.
25. Cristian Bratu, "Mirrors for Princes (Western)," *Handbook of Medieval Studies: Terms – Methods—Trends*, ed. Albrecht Classen (Berlin and New York: Walter de Gruyter, 2010), 2:1921–49.
26. This is powerfully addressed in Bonerius's fable no. 61: "Of a Jew and a Royal Servant (Cupbearer)," where the servant reveals his own crime when he bursts out laughing while carrying a cooked partridge, which reminds him of the live bird that had witnessed his murder of the Jew. The king

then wants to learn the reason for this laughter, and once he has heard the confession, he has the servant executed. Cf. Albrecht Classen, "Laughter as the Ultimate Epistemological Vehicle in the Hands of Till Eulenspiegel," *Neophilologus* 92 (2008): 417–89; see also the contributions to *Laughter in the Middle Ages and Early Modern Times* (see note 4).

27. *La trahison au Moyen Age: de la monstruosité au crime politique (Ve–XVe siècle),* ed. Maïté Billoré and Myriam Soria (Rennes: Presses universitaires de Rennes, 2009); *Treason: Medieval and Early Modern Adultery, Betrayal, and Shame,* ed. Larissa Tracy. Explorations in Medieval Culture, 10 (Leiden and Boston: Brill, 2019); cf. also Albrecht Classen, "Treason: Legal, Ethical, and Political Issues in the Middle Ages: With an Emphasis on Medieval Heroic Poetry," *Journal of Philosophy and Ethics* 1, no. 4 (2019): 13–29; https://www.sryahwa publications.com/journal-of-philosophy-and-ethics/pdf/v1-i4/2.pdf.

28. William C. McDonald, "'Too Softly a Gift of Treasure': A Rereading of the Old High German Hildebrandslied," *Euphorion* 78, no. 1 (1984): 1–16; Wendy Davies, *Acts of Giving: Individual, Community, and Church in Tenth-Century Christian Spain* (Oxford: Oxford University Press, 2007); A.-J. Bujsterveld, *Do ut des: Gift Giving, Memoria, and Conflict Management in the Medieval Low Countries.* Middeleeuwse studies en bronnen, 104 (Hilversum: Verloren, 2007); see also the contributions to *Charity and Giving in Monotheistic Religions,* ed. Miriam Frenkel and Yaacov Lev. Studien zur Geschichte und Kultur des islamischen Orients, N.F., 22 (Berlin and New York: Walter de Gruyter, 2009); Lars Kjær, *The Medieval Gift and the Classical Tradition: Ideals and the Practice of Generosity in Medieval England, 1100–1300.* Cambridge Studies in Medieval Life and Thought. Fourth Series, 114 (Cambridge: Cambridge University Press, 2019).

29. Dante Alighieri, *The Divine Comedy,* vol. I: *Inferno,* trans. with an intro., notes, and commentary by Mark Musa (1977; London: Penguin, 1984), Canto XXXIII, 89.

30. Albrecht Classen, *Freedom, Imprisonment, and Slavery in the Pre-Modern World: Cultural-Historical, Social-Literary, and Theoretical Reflections.* Fundamentals of Medieval and Early Modern Culture, 25 (Berlin and Boston: Walter de Gruyter, 2021), 60–65.

31. Gregory M. Sadlek, *Idleness Working: The Discourse of Love's Labor from Ovid through Chaucer and Gower* (Washington, DC: Catholic University of America Press, 2014).

32. The word "hōustüffel" in Bonerius's text is rare and appears primarily only in the standard lexicon of Swiss-German (under "staffel"), https://digital.idiotikon.ch/idtkn/id10.htm#!page/101411/mode/1up; the word "staffel" combined with "hōu" creates the compound meaning the stalking creature in the hay. In other language areas, "staffel" has a very different meaning. In Marie's fable, "hulchet" was apparently also unusual, as scribal corrections indicate.

33. Albrecht Classen, "Winter as a Phenomenon in Medieval Literature: A Transgression of the Traditional Chronotopos?," *Mediaevistik* 24 (2011): 125–50.

34. Ulrich Boner, *Der Edelstein,* ed. and trans. Stange (see note 5), 383–83; see *Petronii Arbitri Satyricon 100–115, edizione critica e commento,* ed. Giulio Vannini. Beiträge zur Altertumskunde, 281 (Berlin and New York: Walter de Gruyter, 2010). Still valuable proves to be Eduard Grisebach, *Die Wanderung der Novelle von der treulosen Wittwe durch die Weltlitteratur,* 2nd ed. (Berlin: Lehmann, 1889).

35. Romedio Schmitz-Esser, *Der Leichnam im Mittelalter: Einbalsamierung, Verbrennung und die kulturelle Konstruktion des toten Körpers.* Mittelalter-Forschungen, 48. 2nd unchanged ed. (2014; Ostfildern: Jan Thorbecke, 2016), 529–31; see now the English translation by Albrecht Classen and Carolin Radtke as *The Corpse in the Middle Ages: Embalming, Cremation, and the Cultural Construction of the Dead Body* (Turnhout: Harvey Miller Publishers, Brepols, 2020). For a parallel version in fifteenth-century German literature, see *Die Historia von den Sieben weisen Meistern und dem Kaiser Diocletianus.* Nach der Gießener Handschrift 104 mit einer Einleitung und Erläuterungen, ed. Ralf-Henning Steinmetz. Altdeutsche Textbibliothek, 116 (Tübingen: Max Niemeyer, 2001), no. XIV.

36. For many other examples of such a misogynist list of famous men in world history who were abused or deceived by women, see *Woman Defamed and Woman Defended: An Anthology of Medieval Texts*, ed. Alcuin Blamires with Karen Pratt and C. W. Marx (Oxford: Clarendon Press, 1992).

37. *Sir Gawain and the Green Knight: A Dual-Language Version*, ed. and trans. William Vantuono (New York and London: Garland, 1991), 2416–29.

38. Marie de France, *Fables*, ed. and trans. Spiegel (see note 8), 7–8.

University of Arizona
aclassen@email.arizona.edu

Con *Games*

Animal Metaphors, Rhetorics of Seduction and Pedagogies of Consent in the Old French Fabliaux

LUCAS WOOD

Abstract:

In the bawdy, notoriously antifeminist Old French fabliaux, extended animal metaphors for human genitalia exemplify the genre's use of cultivated tensions between literal obscenity and figurative language to map gendered distributions of desire and pleasure onto those of power and knowledge, both erotic and rhetorical. Three case studies explore the ideological flexibility of the genital "animal" as a means of thinking and speaking about men and especially women as desiring, consenting, or resisting erotic agents and subjects so as to affirm the misogynous representational and ideological systems that dominate fabliau discourse or to undermine them from within. In *L'Escuiruel* (*The Squirrel*), animal metaphor serves to endorse misogynous norms and authorize male aggression; in *La Damoisele qui ne pooit oïr parler de foutre* (*The Damsel Who Couldn't Stand to Hear Talk about Fucking*), it participates in reconciling the masculinist desire to "seduce" with women's rhetorically mediated jurisdiction over the legibility and accessibility of their bodies; and *La Sorisete des estopes* (*The Little Mouse in the Oakum*) exploits the ambiguity of linguistic reference to establish the acknowledgment of female consent and pleasure as a precondition for successful masculine performance, both sexual and social.

The Old French fabliaux of the twelfth and thirteenth centuries are notorious as touchstone texts for medieval antifeminism. While hardly kind to men and quite prepared to laugh with women as well as at them, these comic verse vignettes routinely traffic in essentializing clichés about feminine moral failings and generate bawdy, often vicious humor from explicit representations of excessive female sexual appetites and normalized masculine sexual violence.[1] The crudeness of the misogyny

Medievalia et Humanistica, New Series, Number 47 (Reinhold F. Glei and Maik Goth, eds.), Rowman & Littlefield, 2022.

offered up as entertainment and "edification" in many fabliaux corresponds to their blunt, banalizing depiction of coitus, the more frequent, vigorous, and mechanistic the better. However, the pleasures of
obscenity in word and deed—the titillating spectacle of cocks ramming
into cunts (this precise terminology is the currency of the genre's
distinctive aesthetic) and of verbally proliferating *vits* and *cons*—are
often doubled and complemented by the more rarefied gratification
of semiotic play between levels of literal and figurative meaning, locat-
ing the intensity of sexual and textual desire in the complex circuits
linking metaphorical, literal, and physical modes of erotic expression
and enjoyment. Complexity hardly precludes complicity in misogyny's
most virulent discursive and ideological formations, any more than the
narrative liberation and even celebration of female sexuality inhibits
its ultimate condemnation. Games with metaphor do, however, create
the conditions for sophisticated reflection on the multiple rhetorics of
desire and economies of pleasure that run through fabliau narratives,
organizing the relationships between men and women, characters,
writers, and audiences or readers. In experimenting with different ways
of talking about sex, fabliaux pose implicit questions about who can,
does, and should experience desire; how and by whom it is or should be
fulfilled; and under what conditions sexual satisfaction is or should be
available to men and women, independently or mutually. Underscor-
ing the implications of sexual poetics for sexual ethics, the texts also
show how gendered distributions of pleasure are mapped onto those
of power and knowledge, both erotic and linguistic, and are therefore
inextricable from issues of coercion and consent. The results of these
inquiries generate what Carissa Harris dubs "obscene pedagogies,"
ribald narratives that, for better or for worse, instruct characters and
audiences in conceptualizing masculinity and femininity, sexuality and
sex acts, "violence, desire, power, and pleasure."[2]

One provocative cluster of fabliaux articulates its obscene pedagogies
through extended animal metaphors for human genitalia. As means
of indirect reference to sex organs and sex acts, animal metaphors
can dehumanize the sexual subject much as the ubiquitous imagery
of tools, weapons, and household objects tends to do, reducing him
or her to a kind of copulating machine and so sidelining questions of
agency and consent entirely. More often, however, the "comic animali-
sation"[3] of partners and their parts serves to foreground volition and
desire: agricultural implements and craftsmen's tools are there to be
used, but animals have needs and wants, must be tended and tempted,
coaxed and gentled. At the same time, the thematized manipulation

of bawdy metaphor draws attention to the ways in which the creation, comprehension, and control or, on the other hand, the misrecognition, misunderstanding, and clumsy deployment of figurative language can both determine and destabilize gendered power dynamics within the erotic couple.[4] As a resource for thinking and speaking about men and especially women as desiring, consenting, or resisting erotic agents and subjects, the genital "animal" proves to be an ideologically flexible trope. It can, as in *L'Escuiruel* (*The Squirrel*), endorse misogynous norms and authorize sexual aggression, but it is also capable, as in *La Damoisele qui ne pooit oïr parler de foutre* (*The Damsel Who Couldn't Stand to Hear Talk about Fucking*), of reconciling the masculinist desire to "seduce" with women's rhetorically mediated jurisdiction over their bodies' intimate and public legibility and accessibility to men. *La Sorisete des estopes* (*The Little Mouse in the Oakum*) even mobilizes the ambiguity of linguistic reference to establish the acknowledgment of female consent and pleasure as a precondition for male sexual satisfaction—and for the potent performance that the patriarchy itself demands of its disciples.[5] The latter two fabliaux cater to the masculinist perspective encoded in *Escuiruel* in order to co-opt it into their proposition that "one might learn how to please women sexually, to conceive of woman as a desiring subject."[6] While these are at best equivocally "feminist" stories, the characters, voices and narratives they stage can be positioned, like what Jane Burns calls medieval women's literary "bodytalk," "both within and against the social and rhetorical conventions used to construct them."[7] They imagine, with the help of their metaphorical animals and the subtlety that they counterintuitively smuggle into the dehumanizing fabliau model of sexual relations, alternatives to or fissures in the misogynous representational and ideological systems that dominate the fabliaux.

L'Escuiruel

L'Escuiruel, preserved in two manuscript texts considerably divergent in poetic detail but virtually identical in narrative substance, begins with a rich Rouennaise's admonition to her teenage daughter to strictly discipline her speech and especially never to name what hangs between men's legs.[8] Curious about the forbidden thing, the virginal *pucele* (maiden) promptly asks "comment il a a non et qoi" (what it's called and how it's named [*E* 27.5]) and hypothesizes about its identity until her mother is forced to tell her its name, "*vit*." The girl is overheard reveling in her new knowledge by a local youth, Robin, who accosts her and arouses her interest by claiming that the erect penis hidden under his shirt is a squirrel, which she is keen to pet. As she marvels at the warm, quivering "rodent," she encounters Robin's testicles, which he identifies as the squirrel's nest, in which it has laid two eggs with medicinal properties for women. Even more impressed, the girl wishes she had some walnuts to feed the hungry beast; sadly, she ate her whole store yesterday. Fortunately, Robin responds, his squirrel can go up her *con* and find the snack in her stomach. She agrees, Robin throws her down, and the "squirrel" goes looking for walnuts, to her vocal enjoyment and encouragement, until the animal becomes queasy and "vomits" (the narrator says). The girl notices something sticky oozing from her nether regions: the squirrel, she deduces, has broken one of its eggs in the throes of its quest for nuts! This saddens her, but Robin and the "squirrel" are well satisfied as they get up and go on their way.

The fabliau's opening presents it as an exemplary tale about the relationship between linguistic propriety and female social and sexual mores, leading the *B*-text's rubricator to title it *De la mere qui desfandoit sa fille vit a nomer* (*The Mother Who Forbade Her Daughter to Say "Cock"*). A polite lady and especially a nubile maiden, the mother asserts, must watch her tongue and not be

trop fole ne trop vilotiere,	too unruly or licentious,
ne de parler trop prinsautiere,	nor too quick to talk,
car a mal puet en atorner	because people can think ill of
a feme quant en l'ot parler	a woman who is heard speaking
autrement que ele ne doit.	otherwise than as she should.
Por ce chastier se devroit	Therefore, a woman should
feme de parler folement,	refrain from immodest speech,
car il en mesavient sovent.	for misfortune often comes of it.
Sor totes choses garde bien	Above all, take great care
que tu ne nome[s] cele rien	never to name the thing
que cil home portent pendant.	that men have hanging down.

(*E* 17–27)

The first part of this warning pointedly blurs the distinction between *parler* and *parler folement*: in the eyes of an ever-watchful public eager to detect women's misconduct, female speech, as such, risks to be perceived as excessive, condemned as a facet of the "scandalous excess" ascribed to women more generally in the discourse of medieval misogyny, and interpreted as a symptom of the social, moral, and sexual transgression of the dissolute *fole feme* (a common euphemism for the "loose woman" or prostitute).[9] Hence, it seems, the mother's particular proscription of explicit talk about male genitalia. Her concerns anticipate the advice of late fourteenth-century and early fifteenth-century conduct manuals for women. Christine de Pizan's *Livre des Trois Vertus* (*Book of the Three Virtues*) recommends modest, measured "parler ordonné et sage eloquence, non pas mignote mais rassise" (orderly speech and judicious eloquence, composed rather than coquettish), and criticizes "villenie yssue de bouche de dame" (vulgarity coming from a lady's mouth) and "largece de language et d'attraiz accueillans" (liberality with words and inviting manners); *Le Mesnagier de Paris* (*The Parisian Householder*) forbids women to speak "de nulle laidure, non mye seulement de con, de cul ne de autres secretz membres de nature, car c'est deshonneste chose a femme d'en parler" (of anything indecent whatsoever, not only cunts, assholes or other private parts, because it is unseemly for a woman to speak of such things).[10] The word "*vit*," which delicacy keeps the *Mesnagier* (like *Escuiruel*'s mother) from naming even as an example of what women should not say, is surely worst of all because its referent is the assumed object of female desire, as innumerable fabliaux show it to be. To name the phallus publicly is to expose oneself as a "fame . . . de male teche" (woman . . . of bad character [*E* 27.9–27.10]) by avowing a knowledge of it that implies undue interest in or craving for it. Whether motivated by prissy overprotectiveness of a beautiful girl whom "ses pere et sa mere . . . chierissoient / plus que nul des autres enfanz" (her father and mother . . . cherished more than any of their other children [*E* 11–13]), by risible bourgeois pretensions to imitate the genteel behavioral codes of the courtly aristocracy, or by a pragmatic awareness of the material stakes of preserving a marriageable, upwardly mobile girl's reputation, the mother forbids calling a penis what it is in the hopes of protecting her progeny from inadvertently broadcasting to men that she is what she is not: a self-aware wanton seeking to attract male desire by promising its ready reciprocation.

In modeling the use of euphemistic circumlocution to avoid naming "cele peesche / qui entre les jambes pendeille / a ces hommes" (the strip dangling between men's legs [*E* 27.11–27.13]), the sexually experienced mother herself gives credence to the interpretive principle that assumes—perhaps often rightly, if the kind of aggressive linguistic self-policing she advocates is widely practiced—female speech about erotic matters to contain and conceal more knowledge and more desire than it cares to avow.[11] Her daughter's persistent questioning, however, is evidence that at least in this girl's case, language, direct or otherwise, communicates comically less than it lets on. It is true that the *pucele* understands human anatomy (even if she lacks some of the language to designate it) in a purely superficial sense. She is aware that men have something hanging between their legs, and she is familiar with both the physical configuration of her own *con* and the proper word for it, which does not shock her when Robin uses it later on. But her unblinking acceptance of Robin's frank reference to her *con*, not to mention his suggestion that the "squirrel" use it to access the nuts in her stomach, demonstrates what her talk about and around the penis also shows: she is blissfully unaware of any connection between human genitalia, male or female, and sexuality. Despite her mother's efforts to associate male members with *ces hommes* in general, the phallus is for the daughter first and foremost paternal, "la riens que a mon sire / entre les jambes li pent" (the thing hanging between my father's legs [*E* 27.7–27.8]), and thus an attribute of the paradigmatically sexual but also sexually ineligible male. Moreover, the girl's question about the correct term for the phallic "object" quickly becomes curiosity about its function, expressed in conjectural comparisons between the dangling penis and fishing equipment or the fish it catches:

Est ce ore ce dont l'en pesche?	So, is it what one fishes with?
. . . Qu'est ce donc, mere? Est ce loche	. . . What is it, then, mother? Is it a loach
o peson, qui sache plungier	or other fish, able to dive
et noer par nostre vivier	and swim about in our fishpond
et par la fontaine mon pere?	and in my father's pool? (*E* 27.15–33)

These images function as creative metaphors rather than euphemisms insofar as they work, not to overlay and sanitize obscene meaning, but to fill a knowledge gap with generative speculation. They conjure up amusingly incongruous identities for the markedly flaccid male member that ironically and inadvertently (from the girl's, but not the poet's, perspective) resemble standard analogies for sex organs and sexual penetration while disfiguring them to reveal the girl's ignorance and defuse their erotic charge.[12] The dangling, flexible, fishy *peesche* is hardly the meaty, rock-hard, rampant *vit* of a fabliau stud, and although it plunges into a suggestively yonic pond, the *peson* ends up roaming an aquatic habitat that is more naturalized than eroticized.

Filial ignorance, however, does not translate to maternal bliss: the mother's plan to preempt her daughter's initiation into what others will construe as sexual speech has mortifyingly backfired. As if preferring surrender to the embarrassment of entertaining these phallic fantasies and hopeful that a straight answer will dispel the charm of the unknown taboo term, the mother tells the girl that the term for penis is "*vit*." Far from cooling the *pucele*'s excitement, though, the discovery prompts an explosive affirmation of her intent to keep using her new favorite word:

Vit, dist ele, Dieus merci, vit!	"Cock," she said, "thank God, cock!
Vit diré ge, cui qu'il anuit.	I'll say 'cock,' whomever it may offend.
Vit, chaitive! Vit dit mon pere,	'Cock,' wretched woman! My father says 'cock,'
vit dist ma suer, vit dist mon frere,	my sister says 'cock,' my brother says 'cock,'
et vit dist nostre chanberiere;	and our chambermaid says 'cock' too;
et vit avant et vit arriere,	here a 'cock', there a 'cock,'
Vit dist chascuns a son voloir!	everyone says 'cock' to their hearts' content!
Vos meïsmes, mere, por voir dites vit. Et je, fole lasse,	Even you, mother—let's be honest— say 'cock.' And I, poor fool,
qu'é forfet que vit ne nomasse?	what have I done wrong that I shouldn't say 'cock'?
Vit a certes nomerai gié:	I absolutely will say 'cock';
Je meïsmes m'en doinz congié.	I give myself permission. May God give me
Vit me doint Dieus que je n'i faille!	a cock, and I won't fail to do so!"
	(*E* 43–55)

But access to the word "*vit*" does not increase the girl's interest in the thing itself, any more than its frenzied repetition translates the advent of sexual arousal that one might expect.[13] In fact, this sheltered teen-ager's glee, "more linguistic than erotic,"[14] has nothing to do with real penises or men at all, but involves the adolescent pleasure of participation in a (perhaps imagined, since the girl has apparently never heard the word "*vit*" before) linguistic community of worldly adults conceived at the level of her immediate family and household. Her declaration of innocence—what has she done wrong to be denied the right to say "*vit*" like everybody else?—both corresponds to and further proves her sexual innocence insofar as the kind of *forfet* she has in mind is some minor domestic transgression rather than culpable lust. Contrary to what everyone assumes about women's explicit naming of genitalia, the *pucele*'s paroxysm of penis-prattle does not express excessive or even moderate sexual desire because her minimal anatomical and lexical knowledge of the phallus does not extend to an understanding of its use, that is, of the context of gendered and erotic relations between *vits* and *cons* and between men and women into which the linguistic sign and the signifying organ itself are inscribed. When, in closing, she wishes for a cock of her own to call by its true name, she is not asking for a lover, but only for a chance to rebel against her mother by putting her enlarged vocabulary into practice.

Ironically, therefore, although the girl's prayer does call forth a real penis that she will sensationally fail to recognize or designate correctly, the mother's fear that saying "*vit*" will be dangerous for her daughter proves justified for reasons diametrically opposite to those she foresaw. What Robin deduces with "grant joie" (great joy [*E* 70]) from the barrage of "*vits*" he overhears is not that the *pucele* wants a beau or his male member, but that she has no real idea what an erect *vit* is for and that he can exploit her ignorance for his own gratification by calling his cock something else. Only the *A*-text directly identifies Robin as a confirmed trickster who "de barat sot mout et de guile" (was well versed in trickery and guile [E_A 86]), but the *B*-text implies the same point by describing him stroking his *vit* under his shirt until it "forment coloie" (vigorously lifts and bobs its head [*E* 74]), simulating the movements of a frolicsome squirrel. The *A*-text emphasizes that Robin is stimulated, in fact, above all by the prospect of duping the girl: rather than inventing a rhetorical stratagem to satisfy his raging lust for her beautiful body, he deliberately masturbates to erection—"son vit commence a paumoier / tant qu'il l'avoit fet aroidier" (he started to fondle his cock until he got it hard [E_A 95–96])—in order to use his penis as a prop in the rhetorical game of conquest by subterfuge that he desires to stage. Robin calculatingly begins where the mother did by accident and excites his curious target's interest in what he clutches beneath his clothing so that she will ask about it, allowing him to identify it as a squirrel and set her seduction in motion.

Whether *Escuiruel* is read as a "highly misogynistic tale" or a story of "ritualized . . . mutual seduction" celebrating "the erotic power of linguistic artifice" depends largely on whether or not the girl is perceived to see through and willingly play along with Robin's rhetorical recharacterization of his *vit* as an *escuiruel,* taking "knowing and mutual delight in their linguistic acrobatics."[15] The dominant critical consensus unaccountably holds that she does, and is aroused by the *vit*'s metaphorical treatment as she was not by the thing itself or by its proper name, making *Escuiruel* one of a number of fabliau "parables of desire which insist that desire originates in parables."[16] There is no question that the figurative "squirrel" becomes the object of the *pucele*'s desire. In the *A*-text, Robin immediately proposes it as such—"Dame, ce est .i. escuiruel. / Volez le vous?" (Lady, it's a squirrel. Do you want it?)—and she affirms that "Oïl, mon vuel / aus mains le tenisse je ore" (Yes, I'd like to hold it in my hands right now [E_A 103–5]); in the *B*-text, she exclaims spontaneously that "mon vol / l'avroie je a moi joer" (I'd like to have it to play with [*E* 80–81]), and Robin stresses that she can pet the animal at her discretion: "se volez, sel manoiez" (you can stroke it if you like [*E* 88]). However, besides the implausibility of a "comic naïveté" about both sex and oviparous squirrels that finds ample precedent in the fabliau corpus, the text contains no indication that she hankers for Robin's tumescent rod as such and not for his putative tame rodent, squirrels being common pets kept by medieval ladies as well as culturally current sexual symbols.[17] The girl's exchange with her mother subordinated her predilection for metaphor to a push toward the literal, driven by chaste pleasure in associating the signified with its conventional signifier. Moreover, insofar as the metaphorical substitution of *escuiruel* for *vit* does indeed generate and organize a parable of desire, its meaning, like those of all parables, depends on a sustained analogy between two narratives whose exegesis requires precisely an understanding of the narrative relations between things, the structural ways in which they act on and in terms of each other, of which the *pucele* is ignorant when it comes to the *vits* and *cons* that she knows only as unconnected anatomical features of uneroticized male and female bodies. Robin's squirrel metaphor, or, more accurately, his squirrel story, thus scripts a dynamic relationship between genital organs that occurs on the literal level of an erotic parable whose decoded "second sense" (the fabliau's literal account of intercourse) translates his desire alone, just as the parabolic narrative ascribes no supplementary meaning to his partner's body—her *con* remains a *con* whether it is penetrated by a penis or a squirrel—except to the extent that the "nuts" sought in her stomach, which she names and knows literally, become a figure for Robin's sexual satisfaction.

If *Escuiruel* transmits "not so much the narrative account of the sexual act as an account of sexuality that is indissociable from narrative,"[18] that account is initiated and controlled by the rhetorically skilled and sexually aggressive man who directs the action, providing authoritative answers to the *pucele*'s leading questions about how the story unfolds by incorporating the new phenomena she points out. It may be true, strictly speaking, that "no one appears to be victimized"[19] from within the fabliau's diegetic perspective. The girl explicitly consents twice over to the "squirrel's" vaginal quest for nuts—"Metez l'i donques! . . . Certes, jel voil mout volentiers!" (Put it in there, then! . . . Truly, I permit it most willingly! [*E* 130–56])—and cheers the "soueve beste" (delightful animal

[*E* 150]) on to ever more strenuous efforts with repeated expressions of rapture. But although "the girl as passive recipient may take pleasure in the squirrel, . . . she is taken advantage of along the way, and only her conventional compliance keeps the seduction from being a rape."[20] Her physical enjoyment of penetration, which does not preclude a modern evaluation of her experience as sexual assault, is a pleasure without knowledge (like her therefore questionably valid consent) that contrasts with Robin's knowing pleasure and, in a still less savory way, with the pleasure that both he and the narrator take in the asymmetrical distribution of knowledge itself that makes the fabliau a fantasy of masculine linguistic and sexual sway over gullible femininity. Even in a representation of the coital act that is almost uniquely lengthy and detailed in the fabliau corpus,[21] the exhibition of Robin's athletic pumping and prodding at the proffered *con* is subordinate to a pornography of rhetorical domination that plays on the gap between the girl's ignorance, kept in view by the narrator's continued exclusive reference to the penis as "l'escuiruel" throughout the scene, and the smirking superiority that he shares with Robin and with the reader, constituted here—like Robin overhearing the story's opening scene from his "leu secroi" (secret spot [*E* 65])—as an empowered and titillated voyeur.[22] In this respect, *Escuiruel* resembles fabliaux like *Trubert* and *La Grue* (*The Crane*): the former contains a closely analogous scene in which a girl is obliviously pleasured by the penile "pet rabbit" of a man who she thinks is her female companion; the latter shows a sheltered damsel purchasing a young hunter's catch for the price of "un foutre" (a fuck) without knowing what she is trading and then, in the hopes of mollifying her angry governess, trading the *foutre* back to him for the now deliciously prepared bird in order proudly to present herself as "desfoutue" (unfucked).[23]

These tales of dubiously consensual intercourse rely on ludic equivocations of verbal meaning that are undeniably funny, but they center, too, on the crueler humor of ambiguous sexual initiations or seductions that can also signify as sexual violence enacted by linguistic means and enshrined in the power dynamics that structure the stories. In line with the broader fabliau portrayal of a "sexuality that betokens not personal fulfillment, but rivalrous interpersonal struggle,"[24] they construct the apportionment of empowering knowledge and empowered desire as a zero-sum game that men consistently win. If feminine naïveté is humorous, it is one of the devices through which the fabliau, like the pastourelle, works to "make the spectacle of assault tolerable through comic mediation, as it makes the audience complicitous by soliciting its laughter."[25] And if the animal metaphor of *Escuiruel* is arousing, it is so primarily or exclusively for the male seducer, just as its narrative development gratifies mainly male desires, much like the efforts of Robin's "squirrel." After his ejaculation, graphically figured for the reader's delectation or disgust as the animal's crying, spitting, and ultimately vomiting, the girl bemoans what she interprets as the smashing of one of the squirrel's eggs, which puts an apparently premature end to the nut-hunt she has been savoring. Her sorrow at the consequences of Robin's "outrage" (excessive force [*E* 174]) offers yet another of her misunderstood but apt metaphors, this time for her own violent defloration, as Robin departs—the squirrel, he says, has had its fill of nuts, although the girl presses it to look for more—leaving his disappointed conquest with only the "egg" dripping down her thighs.

The misogynous moral about the futility of disciplining female sexual speech appended to the *A*-text is likewise interpretively unsatisfying.[26] *Escuiruel* serves, according to the narrator's hackneyed assertion, to teach

que tels cuide bien chastier	that when someone tries to admonish
sa fille de dire folie,	his daughter against unseemly talk,
et quant plus onques le chastie	the more he admonishes her,
tant le met l'en plus en la voie	the more he pushes her toward
de mal fere . . .	wrongdoing . . . (*E$_A$* 202–6)

Even if women's *dire* can be controlled, their *fere* and the desire that drives it are ungovernable and infinite, probably in part because women love nothing more than bucking (male) authority.[27] This is not a lesson easily learned from an attentive reading of *Escuiruel*. The text does, however, ironically illuminate "the spurious connection between linguistic and sexual purity"[28] in another way that might be read against the grain of the narrator's words. Rather than wanting and having sex without talking about it, the *pucele* talks about the penis, both directly and indirectly, before being penetrated by it without wanting it; and although the mother fails to prevent the utterance of *folie* and the naming of the *vit*, her daughter ends up compromised, not by her own use of language, decorous or otherwise, nor by any lust it might advertise or imply, but by her real innocence and ignorance of sexual matters in word and deed, which leave her vulnerable to the masculinist metaphorics of Robin and his frisky squirrel.

La Damoisele qui ne pooit oïr parler de foutre

Claims about women's capacity to desire and engage in sex without talking about it, at least directly, are better substantiated in *La Damoisele qui ne pooit oïr parler de foutre.* The fabliau survives in three versions across five manuscripts.[29] In the *B* version, on which this analysis will focus, a wealthy farmer's spoiled daughter cannot listen to explicit talk "de foutre / ne de lecherie" (about fucking or lewdness [*D* 6–7]) without becoming nauseated and distressed, preventing her father from employing any male laborers. Hearing of her condition, a young man, David, presents himself at the farm and loudly proclaims that he, too, cannot tolerate terms like "*foutre*," "li moz au deiable" (the devil's word [*D* 90]). The girl insists that her fellow prude be retained and that he sleep in her room, where he promptly engages her in a seductive series of "innocent" questions about her intimate anatomy, which he palpates as he asks her to name each body part. Below her belly, he learns, there is a grassy "pasture" with a "spring" in the middle; past it resides the watchful "trumpeter" who waits to warn off thirsty animals with blasts of his horn. The girl then begins her own tactile and verbal examination of David's genitalia and is introduced to his spirited "colt" and its two attendant "grooms." Since the colt is very hungry and thirsty, the girl invites it to enjoy some grass and then to drink from her spring; if the trumpeter tries to protest, the grooms are welcome to beat him into submission!

The other two variants of *Damoisele* share the same basic plot with some details changed. In the shorter *ACE* version, the girl's father is a baron, the youth is immediately married to her based on his prudish performance, and the erotic catechism, initiated by the girl and beginning with her partner's body (with a "sack of oats" substituted for the twin "grooms"), takes place on their wedding night. In the *D* version, the father is a farmer, but the seducer is a clerk; his deception of the rich *vilain* is more developed, and he makes elaborate protestations of chastity before joining the daughter in bed; and attribution of metaphorical identities to the girl's anatomy begins with her breasts ("sheep's testicles," perhaps game balls made from the dried scrotum) and navel (a "fruit pit," also used in a game like knucklebones) before proceeding to the *con*.[30] The *D*-text alone also concludes with a conventionally misogynous but, in this instance, not unfitting moral to the effect that, where women are concerned, "mout a entre faire et dire" (there is a large gap between doing and saying), leading the *fableor* to argue "que femes n'aient point d'orgueil / de foutre paller hautement / quant il foutent tot igalment" (that women should not disdain to talk out loud about fucking, since they fuck just the same [D_D 224–29]). Few readers would dispute that the tale exposes at least one woman's hypocrisy when it comes to exaggerated linguistic modesty, for it is quite clear, especially in the *B* version, that the female protagonist is one of several fabliau women who "pretend sexual naiveté to cover sexual license."[31] It is far less obvious, however, that the *Damoisele* texts are really "anti-prudery poems"[32] or that this woman fails to profit from a preference for covert desire and oblique speech over unvarnished public talk about fucking. On the contrary, her clever management of the terms in which erotic affairs and eroticized bodies are and are not discussed in her vicinity proves to be a source of power, pleasure, and protection both in the bedroom and in her larger social milieu.

Unlike the girl in *Escuiruel,* the *damoisele* is from the beginning an informed and desiring subject who knows exactly what she blushes to name. Although hearsay holds that she "aoit / les homes et cure n'avoit / ne de lor faiz ne de lor diz" (hated men and had no interest in their doings or words [*D* 37–39]), this is a red herring based on the popular misinterpretation of her famous disdain for men's lewd *diz* as an expression of disinterest in men themselves and their sexual *faiz,* as David seems to sense. Her rejection of foul-mouthed men apparently excludes most of the local population, but it also offers instructions to the one man perceptive enough to hear them. Once David indicates that he has understood what the girl is looking for by elaborately performing his disgust at the word "*foutre*" in her father's courtyard—and the narrator's description of him spitting and grimacing "com s'il aüst mangiee moche" (as if he'd swallowed a fly [*D* 86]) underscores that it is a pantomime put on for her benefit—she runs out to insist that he be hired; at bedtime, she is the one to suggest that, since his morals are above reproach, he should sleep by her side. If David seems forward in immediately reaching for her bare breasts and asking what they are, he once again shows himself adept at reading her cues. Responding to her interest in both intimacy and control, he cedes to her, by adopting the role of "naïve" anatomical ignoramus, the authority to couch their genuinely—and archly self-conscious—mutual seduction in language of her choosing. He continues to follow her lead, getting tacit consent (in the form of her answers to his questions) to each step in the exploration of her body before moving on to the next, as she passes from the literal to the metaphorical register and sets the allegorical scene onto which his "colt" will prance when, after modeling the sort of discourse she wants to hear generated, she poses her own questions and solicits his more active contribution to their "collaborative linguistic and sexual project."[33] And after both partners' pudenda have been comprehensively rechristened, it is the girl who explicitly initiates the imbrication of discrete metaphorical systems and bodies by inviting the "colt" to refresh itself from her "pasture" and "spring" and then by inventing the conceit of the "trumpeter's" drubbing by the "grooms," which brilliantly resolves the problem of her *con*'s "guard" within the allegorical schema so as literally to remove the last (rhetorical) obstacle to intercourse while graphically reconnecting the allegory's fanciful imaginary to the obscene physicality of incipient coitus.

It is noteworthy that *Damoisele*'s metaphors lend only David's *vit* an animal agency implying active volition and desire, while the girl's sexual anatomy becomes a passive landscape of resources to be consumed by the hungry, thirsty "colt." Still, if the stallion is a symbolically virile, phallic animal *par excellence*, the narrative that coalesces around this juvenile horse in search of sustenance focuses more on feminine care than on masculine aggression and gives the *damoisele* absolute control of generously granting the necessitous but not authoritative "animal" what most fabliau men would not hesitate simply to take by force. Moreover, the allegory as such is superintended by the girl and primarily serves her needs. As the text shows when it finally describes how David "li met el con lo vit, / si fait son boen et son talant, / si qu'ele nel tient pas a lant" (put his cock in her cunt and had his way with her in such a manner that she didn't think him a slacker [*D* 204–6]) four times in as many lines of verse, even consensual and mutually enjoyable sex in the fabliaux is almost inevitably a brief, brutal bumping of uglies whose narration makes little space for any real language of female pleasure, although it often takes female desire for granted. Bodies matter as much to the *damoisele* as they do to David, but so does the surplus of enjoyment generated by the flamboyant inappropriateness and implausibility of the analogy between genital organs and landscapes, horses, and human retinues and prolonged by the teasing textual and temporal dilation that metaphor orchestrates. These are the delights that the girl hopes to procure by recruiting and grooming a lover who "a trestote ma meniere" (has mores just like mine [*D* 103]), one well able to take a hint, develop a rhetorical theme, know what needs to be said, and gloss over what should be kept under wraps. It is surely David's mastery of wordplay (and foreplay), which distinguishes him from other men, as much as his groping that brings water to the girl's "fontaine, / qui ne sort mie tot adés" (spring, which doesn't always gush [*D* 148–49]).[34] Putting him through his rhetorical paces before allowing him to pass from words to deeds is a manner of "offering both partners access to a fantasy of masculinity that empowers reciprocal desire," or, to stress the girl's authoritative role, a means of "training a lover to talk in a way which she finds arousing" and then testing him "to find out if he can use the codes which turn her on correctly."[35]

Metaphor, which the *damoisele*'s veto on naming "lecherie, / vit ne coille ne autre chose" (lechery, cocks or balls or whatnot [*D* 22–23]) prescribes for any would-be suitor, thus enables her to (re)define gender and power relations within the intimacy of the couple to her own benefit, although not to the disadvantage of her partner. Beyond establishing the conditions for her narratively and sexually satisfying tryst with David, however, the *damoisele*'s public rejection of lewd language also situates her negotiation of a protected discursive space for female desire in a larger literary and social context. Interpreted as a pretentious attempt by "riche gent" (wealthy folk [*D* 16]) of the peasant class to imitate the linguistic and erotic decorum of their aristocratic betters, the girl's repudiation of explicit talk and the privileging of indirect reference that it necessitates function as the key to a programmatic parody of courtly romance in the *B* version of *Damoisele*.[36] The conquest of a reputedly man-hating "orgoilleuse damoisele" (haughty damsel) analogous to the *orgueilleuses d'amour* of chivalric romance presents a fitting challenge for David, who, like a knight errant, "aloit toz seus par la terre, / comme preuz, avanture querre" (traveled alone throughout the land like a bold, noble man, seeking adventure), albeit less to acquire honor than to "gueaignier son pain" (earn his bread [*D* 35–44]). The girl might also be compared to one of Marie de France's *malmariées*: sequestered with an old male keeper who is all the more unsuitable a match for being her father, her aristocratic-looking alabaster body—"blanche ot la char com flor d'espine" (her flesh was white as the hawthorn blossom [*D* 125])—cries out to be sexually liberated by some lusty youth. Either way, the transparent erotic metaphors with which the barnyard princess and her plebeian paladin simultaneously ennoble and enable their progress toward the baldly reported *foutre* parallel the refined languages of *fin amor* that lead Marie's Guigemar and his lady from kissing to salving love's burning "wound" with the "surplus / de ceo que li altre unt en us" (remainder of what others are wont to do) or help Chrétien de Troyes's Lancelot and Guinevere to discover in each other's arms "des joies . . . la plus eslite" (the sublimest . . . of joys), which "an conte ne doit estre dite" (should not be described in a tale).[37]

Damoisele's staged interference between fabliau discourse and the courtly discourses and motifs it incongruously appropriates to comic effect can amuse its audience on several levels. The appreciation of intertextuality and "intergeneric textuality" is essential to both courtly and fabliau aesthetics, especially in manuscript context.[38] The tale also offers a hilarious send-up of courtly seduction that ironically reveals, as other fabliaux and many "courtly" texts themselves also do, just what indelicate desires and activities the rhetoric of *fin amor* overclothes. But most explicitly, as in *Escuiruel*, the narrator's introduction of his characters and scenario primes the audience to laugh maliciously along with him and with David at the discomfiture and exploitation of the pompous peasant girl and her fatuous father. The ban on lewd language imposed by the

... damoisele,	... damsel,
qui mout par estoit orgoilleuse	who was very haughty
et felonesse et desdaigneuse:	and nasty and supercilious;
que—par foi, je dirai tot outre—	for—by my faith, I'll say it straight out—
ele n'oïst parler de foutre	she could not hear talk of fucking
ne de lecherie a nul fuer,	or lechery of any kind
que ele n'aüst mal au cuer	without becoming nauseated
et trop en faisoit male chiere	and making a great fuss about it
	(*D* 2–9)

is stigmatized as perverse and ridiculous in its social setting, where it makes running her father's farm impossible because no field hand can reasonably be asked to refrain from uttering vulgarities.[39] The father is equally scorned for doting so heavily on the "fille que trop endure" (daughter whom he humors excessively [*D* 31]) that he lets her caprices govern him to the point that "plus ert a li que ele a lui" (he belonged to her more than she to him [*D* 13]).[40] Both are condemned from the perspective of normative misogynous masculinity, the one, like all *orgueilleuses*, for having the gall to shirk her "duty" to prospective suitors by making herself sexually unavailable to men on their terms, the other for letting her get away with such a scandalous dereliction of female duty and sacrificing in the process his (and, symbolically, all) masculine prerogative to control her speech and body while speaking around and about her however the male community sees fit. The audience is thus led to expect, and prepared to enjoy, the story of an uppity woman and her pitifully emasculated guardian getting their comeuppance at the hands of a wily seducer "qui mout savoit barat et guile" (well versed in trickery and guile [*D* 33]) who "uses the girl's sexual ignorance to deflate her social presumption" by turning the "ostentatious performance of social respectability" and verbal decorum that she has solicited against her as punishment for presumptuously thinking that "she has the power to script an elevated form of masculinity to suit her own desires."[41] The narrator's rhyme of "*tot outre*" with "*foutre*" seems to announce his partisan stance on the side of the masculine authority that the text associates with direct, vulgar talk: he will simultaneously spell out the story's premise and its ideological stakes by pronouncing outright the word ("*foutre*") that makes the girl's gorge rise.[42]

As we have seen, however, the outcome of David's encounter with the *damoisele* is not what the audience anticipates, nor is the narrator's antagonism toward his female character as resolute as it initially appears. Over the course of the poem, the narrator does willingly name *vit* and *con*, *coillons* and *foutre*, but he plays this register in counterpoint to different levels of euphemism as well as to the system of extended metaphors generated in the characters' direct discourse. His brusque reintroduction of literal language—"A tant li met el con lo vit" (Thereupon he put his cock in her cunt [*D* 204])—once the "colt" receives permission to drink from the "spring" might be taken to signal David's and the poet's shared triumph over female resistance, but the narrator then revives and, for the first time, participates in the characters' metaphorical system as the poem concludes: "Et se li cornierres groça, / si fu batuz de deus jumaus! / A icest mot faut li flabliaus" (And if the trumpeter objected, he took a beating from the twins! With these words, the fabliau ends [*D* 208–10]). It is telling that the fabliau's final words are figurative ones that combine David's and the *damoisele*'s poetic contributions. Still more interesting is how the narrator introduces the literal sense of what is going on between the two partners immediately before giving free rein to their dialogue and the reader's imagination:

Et Daviez sa main avale   And David slid his hand down
droit au pertuis desoz lo vantre,   straight to the hole under the belly
par o li viz el cors li entre,   through which the cock enters her
                                          body,
si santi les paus qui cressoient . . .   and felt the hair growing there . . .
                                          (*D* 134–37)

His circumlocutory designation of the genital "aperture" is deliberately obscene and aggressively forecasts the still-unwilling girl's inevitable penetration, but it is also a euphemism that allows the poet to respect her wishes, at least insofar as they concern her own rather than the man's body parts, by steering clear of the coarse word *con*, which occurs only once in the poem, until after David receives the girl's unequivocal, if metaphorically articulated, consent to intercourse.

The poem, then, turns out to be much more sympathetic both to figurative language and to female erotic subjects than it first lets on, prompting a reevaluation of the stakes of the narrative and of the repudiation of lewd language that gives rise to it. It is never elucidated whether the *damoisele*'s revulsion at dirty words is really psychosomatic or merely strategic. Regardless, the aversion presented as part of her "nature" (*D* 20) has in fact more to do with the misogynous double bind that medieval (and modern) culture imposes on the public display of female sexuality, which is hypocritically at once demanded and stigmatized by men—such that the *damoisele* is criticized for adopting voluntarily the exact policy of linguistic puritanism that her analogue in *Escuiruel* was urged to observe. Even the girl's father, the only victim of his daughter's and David's collaborative *guile* and the ultimate butt of the fabliau's joke, complains about her inconvenient prudishness but would also surely object to her sleeping with the help. Far from being some kind of erotic disability, the *damoisele*'s intolerance of obscene language creates perhaps the only conditions under which a nubile girl would be allowed to manage her own sexual accessibility in both positive and negative ways. On the one hand, it allows her to deflect unwanted male attention on a daily basis: her "condition," which prevents her father from hiring foul-mouthed menservants, effectively eliminates potential sexual harassers from her home environment. On the other hand, it lulls paternal suspicion to the point that she can take the lover of her choice into her bedroom with her father's complacent encouragement to follow her "volanté . . . do tot" (inclination . . . entirely [*D* 118–19]). Only her personified anus—a farcical confederate of Dangier, Male Bouche, Honte and Peur, the figures of parental and social oversight and of the internalized self-policing it inculcates who guard the virginal rosebud in Guillaume de Lorris's *Roman de la Rose*[43]—stands in the way of sexual gratification on, and in, her own terms.[44]

Damoisele does not envision unmitigated sexual agency and freedom for women. Female desire, or at least its acceptable expression, remains subject to the constraints of secrecy and compulsory euphemism, delectable though they may be. Moreover, the text's camouflaging of a story strikingly sympathetic to women beneath the trappings of a masculinist seduction plot akin to *Escuiruel*'s dramatizes how affirmations of the value of feminine consent and pleasure, especially by women themselves, need to be "euphemized" on a narrative level and made contingent on the partnership—and the pleasure—of a man. But it also gives *Damoisele* a subtlety that distinguishes it from other fabliaux that foreground animal metaphors' capacity to enable and enrich women's erotic lives, allowing them to "maintain the appearance of outward propriety and be sexually fulfilled at the same time."[45] Both *Porcelet* (*Piggie*) and its cognate *La Dame qui aveine demandoit pour Morel sa provende avoir* (*The Lady Who Asked for Blackie to Be Fed His Oats*) introduce happily married couples who invent allegories of intercourse that invert *Damoisele*'s, metaphorizing the *con* as a hungry piglet or horse and the *vit*, or the "seed" it dispenses, as the animal's sustenance.[46] This facilitates so much sex, initiated by the wives' invocation of the arousing figurations, that their husbands' stores of "wheat" or "oats" are depleted. Emasculated and embittered, the men finally rebel at "feeding time" by farting or defecating in their wives' laps; there is no "grain" left, and their voracious cunts will have to make do with the bran (a filthy pun: Old French "*bran*" means both grain husks and excrement). In *Porcelet* and *Morel*, rhetorically empowered female desire overplays its hand, leading to a fracturing of metaphorical signification that reduces figurative language to foul wind and reasserts male power over verbal meaning and sexual life under the banner of resentful misogyny. *Damoisele*, on the other hand, allows its protagonist's fantasy to coexist with that other, antifeminist fantasy animating *Escuiruel*, leaving an interpretive out for the masculinist reader that functions as an escape valve for misogyny's pressure on both the clever girl and her tale.

La Sorisete des estopes

The defense of women's sexual control over (access to) their own bodies that is at the heart of *La Sorisete des estopes* not only coexists with the misogyny that the text expects from its audience, but more concertedly exploits the structures of misogynous thought against themselves. Like *Escuiruel*, this fabliau uses a specious equivalency between animals and genitals to negotiate the asymmetrical distribution of sexual knowledge and power within a couple, but in *Sorisete*, the gender positions are reversed on every level. The sole surviving manuscript text introduces

. . . un vilain sot,	. . . a stupid peasant
qui fame prist et rien ne sot	who took a wife, knowing nothing
de nul deduit q'apartenist	of any pleasures germane to
a fame se il la tenist,	a wife if he had one,
c'onques entremis ne s'en fu.[47]	for he'd never been involved in them.

(*S* 1–5)

His new bride, on the other hand, knows all about men and the fun to be had with them, being the mistress of the local priest, who begs to enjoy her favors one last time before her husband exercises his marital rights. Accordingly, when the *vilain* comes to bed and begins to investigate female anatomy, she tells him that he will not find her *con*, which she has absentmindedly left at her parents' house. The wife trysts with the priest while her husband treks to the next town and receives from his mother-in-law (who is not in on the joke, but deduces that her daughter is up to something) a basket of flax or hemp oakum that supposedly contains the missing orifice.[48] Impatient with lust, the *vilain* stops partway home to stick his penis into the basket, causing a mouse that has (unbeknownst to everyone) nested there to leap out and flee into the dew-wet grass as the man vainly begs for the return of what he thinks is his wife's *con*. Arriving home and climbing disconsolately back into bed, the *vilain* admits that he has lost the *con*, but his wife reassures him that it has run back to its proper place between her legs and proceeds to show him how to gently touch and hold the timid beast so that it will not run away again.

Simon Gaunt asserts, somewhat contradictorily, that *Sorisete* offers "the ultimate affront to male dignity" but "does not have an overt political agenda," although "the husband's chase of his wife's elusive *con* aptly figures the manner in which her sexuality escapes his control."[49] The text explicitly begs to differ; it does have something to say about gender politics, inspired precisely by the threat to male dignity and authority posed by the runaway *con* and summed up in the narrator's parting lesson that men must stay vigilant against their wives' feminine wiles because

. . . fame set plus que deiable . . .	. . . a woman knows more than the devil . . .
Qant ele viaut om decevoir,	When she wants to trick a man,
plus l'en deçoit et plus l'afole	she hoodwinks and mystifies him more
tot solemant par sa parole	with her words alone
que om ne feroit par angin.	than a man could with best-laid plans. (*S* 214–21)

Diabolical ingenuity is hardly necessary to dupe a dolt as ignorant as the man in the tale, but the misogynous truism that women deceive men for their own nefarious ends is easy to discern in the fabliau's first act, where the bride sends her husband on a wild cunt chase so that she can rendezvous with the lecherous priest. It does not, however, account for the fortuitous coincidence of the mouse's presence in the oakum basket or the misidentification of the rodent as the wife's *con*, an error entirely of the husband's devising on which the narrative hinges and both its main joke and its "obscene pedagogy" turn. The unforeseeable substitution of animal for *con* allows the text, following the trail of the *sorisete*, to escape the control of its misogynous frame, scamper off the well-trodden narrative path leading the unenlightened *vilain* back to the grotesque consummation of an unhappy marriage, and find its way to a political agenda far more favorable to women—and an ending that looks unexpectedly like conjugal harmony.

The foundations for these developments are laid, however, when the *vilain* first blunders into the nuptial bed. His wife's resistance to his inept advances is explicitly motivated by an adulterous preference for her tonsured paramour, but it is described as self-defense against marital rape:

Et il la prant entre ses braz,	And he seized her in his arms
si l'anbraça mout duremant	and clutched her very hard
—que il nel sot faire autremant—	—for he knew no better—
et l'a mout soz lui estandue;	and forced her down flat beneath him;
et cele s'est mout desfandue	and she defended herself strenuously,
et dist: "Qu'est ce que volez faire?"	saying: "What are you trying to do?" (*S* 28–33)

The husband's answer—"Je voil . . . vit avant traire, / si vos fotrai se j'onques puis, / se vostre con delivre truis" (I want . . . to get out my cock and fuck you if I can, if I find your cunt unencumbered [*S* 34–36])—expresses his inability to conceive of women as erotic subjects as well as his ignorance of the mechanics of intercourse. Not only is he oblivious to his partner's dismay at his violent "seduction," he fails meaningfully to connect the wife to whom he talks with the anatomical *con* he hopes to fuck, *cons* being, in his blinkered semantic system, primarily things that new husbands finally get to *foutre* at will and for their own pleasure on their wedding nights. Quick-wittedly exploiting the man's weak grasp of deictic reference and his objectification of the sexualized female body, the woman therefore protects herself by drawing out the consequences of the principle he proposes: women and *cons* are two separate things, so while all women own *cons*, they might sometimes forgetfully leave home without them. "Cunning speech successfully enables escape from her conjugal duty in sex," at least for the time being.[50] In fact, whether or not the *vilain* and his bride are really already married, and hence whether or not the obligation to pay the conjugal debt is in force, is quite controversial from the standpoint of canon law. According to Gratian, the marital debt requires both spouses to provide sex whenever either one of them requests it, but only after the consummation of their marriage by an act of intercourse that is presumably voluntary and not owed, although other canonists hold that present consent to marriage is sufficient to forge the bonds of matrimony. From either perspective, in deflecting the *vilain*'s violent advances either before his legal right to her favors is initiated or else on its first invocation, his bride rejects his approach to conjugal sexuality on grounds that canon law might accept if she is viewed as a near-victim of sexual assault rather than a scheming adulteress. While medieval "canonists refused to admit the possibility that a husband could rape his wife," Gratian holds that marriage, as opposed to mere "casual cohabitation," should be governed by a "marital affection" involving "a habitual attitude of respect, deference, and consideration toward one's spouse."[51]

Whether or not the *fableor* or his audience are versed in canon law, the wedding night's postponement makes time for the *vilain*'s first lesson in how to approach women, administered, ironically, through a second failed rape attempt amusingly free of female victims. As he works himself up to fuck the *con* that he thinks is tucked away in the basket of oakum, the *vilain* unwittingly prepares to confound it with the mouse by constructing it as an animal. Having heard the *con* figured by other men (or perhaps in fabliaux, which also often feature and fetishize genitals detached from human bodies) as a little beast, he wants, he says, to "savoir se c'est voirs o non / que l'an dit, que il a en con / mout doce et mout soef beste" (find out if it's true or not what they say, that the cunt is a very sweet and pleasant animal [*S* 89–91]). Still struggling with linguistic reference, he takes the popular metaphor literally, wondering "se dort o voille / li cons ma fame" (if my wife's cunt is asleep or awake [*S* 82–83]) and worrying that, if disturbed, it might get out of its basket and run away. These qualms do not prevent him from thrusting his erect *vit* into the basket in a parody of rape (or fabliau sex, which often looks much the same), but they do suggest a dim awareness that the drowsy or fearful—and, as is grammatically appropriate, feminized—*beste* might not be in an amorous mood that contrasts with the man's total failure to consider his wife's disposition before leaping on top of her. His inkling seems confirmed when the molested mouse scurries off into the fields. The small and delicate thing is, he gathers, upset about being jabbed by his big, ugly, black *vit* with its menacing red "musel" (muzzle [*S* 111]); the *vit*, too, is implicitly animalized, as is the man himself, whose dismayed grimaces resemble "la moe / que li singes fait qant il rit" (the face a monkey makes when it laughs [*S* 126–27]). "Je cuit certes," he concludes, "qu'ele ait peor / de mon vit" (I'm sure it was frightened of my cock [*S* 108–9]), and his futile plea for the cunt-mouse's return accordingly includes both verbal blandishments and a promise to respect its sexual autonomy:

Biaus cons, doz cons, tost revenez!	Fair cunt, sweet cunt, come back quickly!
Tote ma fiance tenez	I give you my solemn word
que mais ne vos adeserai	that I'll make no attempts on you
devant que a l'ostel serai	before I get back home
et tant que vos avrai livré	and return you
a ma fame . . .	to my wife . . . (*S* 129–34)

The mouse, not so much a metaphor for the cunt as a placeholder for it that "unsettles the connection between signifier and signified in the refer-ent 'con,'"[52] lends the displaced site of female sexuality an elusive animal agency or volition. It sidesteps the man's sexual aggression and remains defiantly deaf and dumb in the face of his apologetic supplication, the inverted reflection of his silent failure to engage his wife verbally before assailing her body. Standing outside the structures of power in which men and women are caught up, and in which men can demand satisfaction of women, the cunt-mouse helps the *vilain* both to fathom why a woman might fear or flee the unsolicited thrusts of his *vit* and to begin to imagine a female erotic agency that defies his manly prerogatives and denies him gratification unless it is taken into account. And if the *con*'s return to its owner marks the term of the *vilain*'s proposed truce with it, his vow also starts to acknowledge his wife as the rightful mistress of the *beste*.

Trudging home cuntless, the dispirited peasant pictures a lifetime of sexless marriage: by losing the *con*, he has voided the conjugal debt. In-deed, although his wife's dalliance with the priest has gone better than his with the mouse, the *vilain*'s attempt at intercourse with someone, or something, that he views as other than his wife leaves him, too, in the po-sition of the adulterer, who forfeits the right to invoke the conjugal debt according to canon law.[53] Back in the conjugal bed, however, the *vilain* demonstrates that his lesson has not quite sunk it. His wife, not knowing what *con* can possibly have been "lost" but inferring that her husband's ignorant sexual aggression is involved, aptly reiterates the principle that *cons* dislike rude men who have not properly made their acquaintance. Nevertheless, asked how he would proceed given a second chance, the *vilain* voices a violent fantasy that belies his restraint with regard to his wife's supposedly epicene body:

Je lo foutroie, par ma foi!	Why, I'd fuck it, by my faith,
Et voir en l'oil li boteroie,	and ram it right in the eye
ensi que je lo creveroie	hard enough to blind it
por lo coroz que il m'a fait!	for the trouble it's given me! (*S* 182–85)

If the husband now has some idea of what not to do with *cons*, he has no positive knowledge of their tastes, and once again, ignorance, aggravated by humiliated vindictiveness, fuels his sexual belligerence. Carefully, then, calling the *con* by its proper masculine pronoun (as opposed to the feminine one that denoted *la beste*) in a way that perhaps encourages her husband to respect its wants and needs while also distancing the *con* from herself so as to underscore its feral autonomy and glorify her vital intermediary role as a vagina whisperer, she shows him how to calm and cosset the wild cunt with soft caresses: "Or l'aplaigniez don tot au mains . . . qu'il ne vos estorde, / et n'aiez peor qu'il vos morde" (Smoothly stroke it a bit now . . . so that it doesn't twist away from you, and have no fear that it will bite you [*S* 194–96]).[54] It is now the husband who might be leery of the metaphorically animalized *con* rather than vice versa, but of course, it refrains from using its teeth, and the man repays its docility in kind: since it is surely exhausted and palpably very wet from its adventures in the dewy fields, he says, he will let it rest tonight rather than taking things any further, "que ne vos voil hui mais grever" (for I don't want to bother you any more this day [*S* 211]). This is not a permanent renunciation, nor does the wife advocate one. A husband who lies silently in bed with his back to her may be better than a rapist, but he cannot meet the needs that the woman, after her last hurrah with the priest, is now prepared to satisfy in the marriage bed. But the *vilain's* newfound consideration for the drenched, tired *con* forecasts a future in which his wife's favors will be understood less as his due to be claimed than as something to desire and negotiate for in a modest, respectful manner attuned to her volition and pleasure, even if they are attributed to the *doce beste* nestled between her legs.[55]

The conflation of *sorisete* and *con* thus ultimately contributes to correcting, at least preliminarily, the *vilain's* inability or unwillingness to understand women as desiring subjects and sexual agents. The wife appears never to discover what happened on her husband's way home or what he thinks a *con* is. She simply knows her husband's proclivities and capitalizes on his evident confusion to teach him about consent, foreplay, and female pleasure—a pleasure unlike those represented in *Escuiruel* and *Damoisele*, and exceptional in a fabliau, in that it is not phallocentric—in terms that happen to apply both (mostly metaphorically) to her real genitalia and (mostly literally) to the mouse that he has mistaken for them. The husband, meanwhile, is stubbornly, absurdly unaware that any figurative language is being used at all. For him, his wife's real "anatomy—along with her desires, her fear—remains invisible"[56] to the end. The literal, composite cunt-mouse functions as a kind of filter or translation tool that makes his wife's literal lesson about women comprehensible as a tutorial on how to deal with a small furry animal whose subjectivity is easier for him to grasp, and over which he is less socially compelled to assert his virile power.

As the fabliau concludes, the audience is still laughing, as it has been all along, at the *vilain sot*—"Onques plus fous ne fu veüz!" (A dafter one was never seen [*S* 58]), the narrator sneers—and with his astute, unflappable wife. Introduced in the triply damning opening sentence as an idiot, an adult male virgin and a cuckold, then depicted failing to find or fuck his wife's *con*, confusing it with a mouse, and finally losing control over even the rodent in a way that ends up definitively reversing the sexual power dynamic within his marriage, the *vilain* is right about one thing: "Faite en sera mout grant risee" (I will become a laughingstock [*S* 136])! Like the father and daughter in *Damoisele*, the *vilain* is set up to be roundly condemned from the standpoint of normative masculinity. Masculinist readers want to identify with smooth-tongued, hard-pricked ladykillers like Robin and David, not an ignoramus incapable of understanding, mastering, or satisfying a woman. Textualized misogyny, of course, does not depend on favorable representations of men, and many fabliaux subject masculine as well as feminine libidos and inappropriate sexual performances to "painful discipline," but mockery of stupid or inadequate men typically reaffirms ideals of authoritative, potent masculinity and prescribes proper masculine "sexual dominance."[57] *Sorisete*'s derision of the *vilain*, however, refigures marital rape and fabliau sexual violence more generally, which almost invariably function to express male power and invite cruel laughter at women's degrading and traumatic domination, as symptoms of disempowering male ignorance and impotence. In order to avoid the *vilain*'s humiliation in the eyes of both men and women, the misogynous reader learns, he too must restrain his most brutal urges, maintain a wary respect for female sexual autonomy, and make space for female sexual pleasure, which is after all congruent with his own. *Sorisete* thus ingeniously recruits its male audience into a didactic program that harnesses the misogynous structures of normative masculinity itself to reroute a cynical, masculinist "obscene pedagogy" in a self-undermining direction. And the conclusion of the tale suggests that—at least for the *vilain*, but perhaps also for *Damoisele*'s David, who "seduces" his singularly knowing ingénue by submitting to a voluptuous renaming of his body and a rescripting of his desire—relinquishing what Holly Crocker calls the "burden of normative masculinity" committed to sexual mastery and "defined by its regulatory relation to feminized desire" can come as a relief and even, eventually, a pleasure of its own.[58]

Notes

1. See Norris J. Lacy, *Reading Fabliaux* (New York: Garland, 1993), 60–77, and Per Nykrog, *Les Fabliaux*, 2nd ed. (Geneva: Droz, 1973), 193–207. The facts that misogyny is incidental in many fabliaux, that the failings of various types of men as well as women are stereotyped, mocked, and cruelly punished in these texts, and that *fableors* readily acknowledge female agency, power, wit, and resourcefulness and align their narrative perspectives with those of female characters, as shown by Lesley Johnson, "Women on Top: Antifeminism in the Fabliaux?," *Modern Language Review* 78, no. 2 (1983): 298–307, do not controvert the general, underlying antifeminism of the corpus. However, the nuanced complexity of fabliau constructions of women, gender, and gender hierarchy is explored by E. Jane Burns, *Bodytalk: When Women Speak in Old French Literature* (Philadelphia: University of Pennsylvania Press, 1993), 27–70; Simon Gaunt, *Gender and Genre in Medieval French Literature* (Cambridge: Cambridge University Press, 1995), 234–85; Holly Crocker, "Disfiguring Gender: Masculine Desire in the Old French Fabliau," *Exemplaria* 23, no. 4 (2011): 342–67; Philippe Ménard, *Les Fabliaux: Contes à rire du Moyen Âge* (Paris: Presses Universitaires de France, 1983), 131–40; and Natalie Muñoz, *Disabusing Women in the Old French Fabliaux* (New York: Peter Lang, 2014). The vexed and often tautological question of the fabliau's defining generic characteristics and boundaries is also nearly inextricable from the evaluation of "fabliau" texts' literary ideologies where the representation of love, sex, and women is concerned.
2. Carissa M. Harris, *Obscene Pedagogies: Transgressive Talk and Sexual Education in Late Medieval Britain* (Ithaca: Cornell University Press, 2018), 25.
3. Brian J. Levy, *The Comic Text: Patterns and Images in the Old French Fabliaux* (Amsterdam: Rodopi, 2000), 58.
4. The poetic and power dynamics of fabliaux are often defined by the relationships between and shifting positions of the dupers and the duped; see Mary Jane Stearns Schenck, *The Fabliaux: Tales of Wit and Deception* (Amsterdam: John Benjamins, 1987), 71–92, and Corinne Denoyelle, "Le Discours de la ruse dans les fabliaux: Approche pragmatique et argumentative," *Poétique* 115 (1998): 327–50.
5. At least a few medieval readers had the opportunity to compare these fabliaux: all three are preserved in ms. Bern, Burgerbibliothek, 354.
6. Burns, *Bodytalk*, 45.
7. Burns, *Bodytalk*, 7.
8. *L'Escuiruel*, published as *L'Esquiriel*, in *Nouveau Recueil complet des fabliaux (NRCF)*, ed. Willem Noomen and Nico van den Boogaard, 10 vols. (Assen: Van Gorcum, 1983–1998), 6:33–49, 319–22. *Escuiruel* appears in mss. Paris, BnF, fr. 837, fols. 333ra–334ra (ms. *A*), and Bern, Burgerbibliothek, 354, fols. 39va–41ra (ms. *B*). Parenthetical references marked *E* give line numbers in the critical edition, based on the *B*-text; E_A and E_B respectively distinguish references to the diplomatic editions of the *A*- and *B*-texts, which I punctuate and emend as necessary. All English translations of medieval French texts in this essay are my own.
9. See R. Howard Bloch, *Medieval Misogyny and the Invention of Western Romantic Love* (Chicago: University of Chicago Press, 1991), especially 14–22.
10. Christine de Pizan, *Le Livre des Trois Vertus*, ed. Charity Cannon Willard and Eric Hicks (Paris: Honoré Champion, 1989), 45, 133; *Le Menagier de Paris*,

ed. Georgine E. Brereton and Janet M. Ferrier (Oxford: Clarendon Press, 1981), 129. I borrow these comparisons from Lisa Perfetti, "The Lewd and the Ludic: Female Pleasure in the Fabliaux," in *Comic Provocations: Exposing the Corpus of Old French Fabliaux*, ed. Holly A. Crocker (New York: Palgrave Macmillan, 2006), 23–24 [17–31]. Similar warnings against excessive and unseemly speech appear in *Le Livre du Chevalier de la Tour Landry pour l'enseignement de ses filles*. On the convergence of conduct manuals' and fabliaux's concerns about language, see also Danielle Bohler, "Civilités langagières: Le *bon taire* ou le *parler hastif*. Brèves réflexions sur la fonction sociale et symbolique du langage," in *Norm und Krise von Kommunikation: Inszenierungen literarischer und sozialer Interaktion im Mittelalter*, ed. Alois Hahn, Gert Melville, and Werner Röcke (Berlin: LIT, 2006), 115–33.

11. Indeed, the *B*-text has the mother herself refer, in a couplet that the editor rightfully rejects as dissonant in context, to "cele rien / que cil home portent si grant, / que nos femes amommes tant" (the thing that is so big on men, which we women love so much [E_B 26–28]).

12. Similarly, the girl will exclaim, upon touching Robin's supposedly ailing "squirrel," that "il est toz vis" (he is quite lively [*E* 97]); from the reader's perspective, she unwittingly puns on the near-homophony between "vif" (lively) and "vit" (cock) in a way that amusingly underscores her failure to realize that the squirrel is in fact a penis.

13. Nor, however, does repetition serve to *de*-eroticize the obscene word—as is asserted by R. Howard Bloch, *The Scandal of the Fabliaux* (Chicago: University of Chicago Press, 1986), 86; Lacy, *Reading Fabliaux*, 81–82; and Miranda Griffin, "Dirty Stories: Abjection in the Fabliaux," *New Medieval Literatures* 3 (2000): 249 [229–60]—since it never held an erotic charge for the girl to begin with.

14. Lacy, *Reading Fabliaux*, 81.

15. Caroline Jewers, "*L'Esquiriel*, or What's in a Tail?," in *The Old French Fabliaux: Essays on Comedy and Context*, ed. Kristin L. Burr, John F. Moran, and Norris J. Lacy (Jefferson, NC: McFarland, 2007), 72 [69–81]; Lacy, *Reading Fabliaux*, 83–84; Perfetti, "The Lewd and the Ludic," 26.

16. Bloch, *Scandal*, 90–91; see also R. Howard Bloch, "Modest Maids and Modified Nouns: Obscenity in the Fabliaux," in *Obscenity: Social Control and Artistic Creation in the European Middle Ages*, ed. Jan M. Ziolkowski (Leiden: Brill, 1998), 297–99 [293–307]; Alexandre Leupin, *Barbarolexis: Medieval Writing and Sexuality* (Cambridge, MA: Harvard University Press, 1989), 93; and Crocker, "Disfiguring Gender," 361–63.

17. The girl's "naïveté comique" is a "fausse naïveté," according to Rosanna Brusegan, "La Naïveté comique dans les fabliaux à séduction," in *Comique, satire et parodie dans la tradition renardienne et les fabliaux: Actes du colloque des 15 et 16 janvier 1983*, ed. Danielle Buschinger and André Crépin (Göppingen: Kümmerle, 1983), 23 [19–30]. On medieval pet squirrels, see Kathleen Walker-Meikle, *Medieval Pets* (Woodbridge: Boydell, 2012), 48–52; on the squirrel in erotic iconography, see Lucy Freeman Sandler, "A Bawdy Betrothal in the Ormesby Psalter," in *Tribute to Lotte Brand Philip: Art Historian and Detective*, ed. William W. Clark et al. (New York: Abaris, 1985), 154–59; Michael Camille, *The Medieval Art of Love: Objects and Subjects of Desire* (New York: Harry N. Abrams, 1998), 103–4; and Michael Camille, *Mirror in Parchment: The Luttrell Psalter and the Making of Medieval England* (Chicago: University of Chicago Press, 1998), 299. Some bestiary traditions also associate the squirrel with the "base" sense of touch and characterize it, on the basis of

its lifestyle and habits, as lazy, concupiscent, greedy, and foolish; see Michel Pastoureau, "Le Bestiaire des cinq sens (XIIe–XVIe siècle)," *Micrologus* 10 (2002): 142–44 [133–45].

18. Bloch, *Scandal,* 87.
19. Roy J. Pearcy, "Modes of Signification and the Humor of Obscene Diction in the Fabliaux," in *The Humor of the Fabliaux: A Collection of Critical Essays,* ed. Thomas D. Cooke and Benjamin L. Honeycutt (Columbia: University of Missouri Press, 1974), 177 [163–96]; see also Roy J. Pearcy, *Logic and Humour in the Fabliaux: An Essay in Applied Narratology* (Cambridge: D. S. Brewer, 2007), 56. The same viewpoint is espoused by Crocker, "Disfiguring Gender," 361–62, and Muñoz, *Disabusing Women,* 114.
20. Jewers, "*L'Escuiriel,*" 78.
21. Bloch, "Modest Maids," 295.
22. The complicity of *fableor* and audience can be seen to create an Old French version of the misogynous, homosocial Middle English "felawe masculinity" described by Harris, *Obscene Pedagogies,* 26–66. A similar culture might have been fostered by the medieval Latin schoolroom's pedagogical use of texts about rape, examined by Marjorie Curry Woods, "Rape and the Pedagogical Rhetoric of Sexual Violence," in *Criticism and Dissent in the Middle Ages,* ed. Rita Copeland (Cambridge: Cambridge University Press, 1996), 56–86.
23. *Trubert,* in *NRCF,* 10:143–262, 360–75 (see vv. 2472–565 in the critical edition); *La Grue,* published with its Anglo-Norman analogue *Le Heron,* under the title *Cele qui fu foutue et desfoutue,* in *NRCF,* 4:151–87, 395–402. On *Trubert*'s intertextual relationship with *Escuiruel* (and perhaps, less directly, with *Damoisele* as well), see Roy J. Pearcy, "Fabliau Intertextuality: Some Connections between Related Comic Narratives," *Reinardus* 20 (2007–2008): 57–62 [51–66]. *Grue* is one of the few fabliaux in which a sexually exploited woman complains explicitly about her partner's (or assailant's) roughness as he searches for his *foutre* under her skirts: "Vaslez, tu quiers trop durement!" (My lad, you're foraging too hard! [v. 84 in the critical edition]).
24. Sarah Melhado White, "Sexual Language and Human Conflict in Old French Fabliaux," *Comparative Studies in Society and History* 24, no. 2 (1982), 185 [185–210]. Cf. the related discussion of power struggles within fabliau marriages in Philippe Ménard, "Les Conflits de pouvoir dans les fabliaux," in *Penser le pouvoir au Moyen Âge (VIIIe–XVe siècle),* ed. Dominique Boutet and Jacques Verger (Paris: Rue d'Ulm/Presses de l'École normale supérieure, 2000), 171–80.
25. Kathryn Gravdal, *Ravishing Maidens: Writing Rape in Medieval French Literature and Law* (Philadelphia: University of Pennsylvania Press, 1991), 115.
26. On the challenges of interpreting fabliau morals, see Lacy, *Reading Fabliaux,* 144–49.
27. This is one lesson of *La Dame escoillee* (*The Gelded Lady*), in *NRCF,* 8:1–125, 347–60.
28. Perfetti, "The Lewd and the Ludic," 25.
29. *La Damoisele qui ne pooit oïr parler de foutre,* in *NRCF,* 4:57–89, 374–79. *Damoisele* appears in mss. Paris, BnF, fr. 837, fols. 182va–183ra (ms. *A*); Bern, Burgerbibliothek, 354, fols. 58ra–59vb (ms. *B*); Berlin, Staatsbibliothek, Ham. 257, fol. 45ra–va (ms. *C*); Paris, BnF, fr. 19152, fols. 55rb–56ra (ms. *D*); and Paris, BnF, fr. 1593, fol. 185ra–vb (ms. *E*). Parenthetical references marked *D* give line numbers in the critical edition of the *B*-text (*NRCF*'s "version II"); D_{ACE} and D_D, respectively, distinguish references to the critical edition of the *ACE*-text (*NRCF*'s "version I") and the diplomatic edition of

the *D*-text (*NRCF*'s "version III"), which I punctuate and emend as necessary. The three versions of *Damoisele* are compared by Gaunt, *Gender and Genre*, 280–84; Jean Rychner, *Contribution à l'étude des fabliaux: Variantes, remaniements, dégradations*, 2 vols. (Neuchâtel/Geneva: Faculté des lettres/Droz, 1960), 1:84–91; and Sophie Marnette, "Framing Discourse: Three Versions of *De la damoisele qui ne pooit oïr parler de foutre*," in *"Si sai encor moult bon estoire, chançon moult bone et anciene": Studies in the Text and Context of Old French Narrative in Honour of Joseph J. Duggan*, ed. Sophie Marnette, John F. Levy, and Leslie Zarker Morgan (Oxford: Society for the Study of Medieval Languages and Literatures, 2015), 199–220.

30. These details accentuate the importance of games and gaming, whose thematic and structural centrality to the fabliau is remarked by Clarissa Bégin, "Le Fabliau, genre didactique (Étude sur *La Damoisele qui ne pooit oïr parler de foutre*)," *Reinardus* 16 (2003): 19–29.

31. Crocker, "Disfiguring Gender," 354; see also Brusegan, "Naïveté comique."

32. Charles Muscatine, *The Old French Fabliaux* (New Haven: Yale University Press, 1986), 141. Muscatine sees fabliau obscenity as caught up in a discursive agon with emergent courtly codes of verbal decorum.

33. Lacy, *Reading Fabliaux*, 118n.

34. The girl makes the opposite observation about her "spring" in the *D*-text: "toz jors sort et ja n'ert pleine" (it flows constantly but never fills up [D_D 158]).

35. Crocker, "Disfiguring Gender," 360; Gaunt, *Gender and Genre*, 282. The girl in the *ACE* version delightedly emphasizes that her partner is a quick study: "Sire, mout estes bien apris!" (My lord, you've learned your lessons well! [D_{ACE} 68]).

36. Keith Busby, "Courtly Literature and the Fabliaux: Some Instances of Parody," *Zeitschrift für romanische Philologie* 102 (1986): 80–81 [68–87]; Roy J. Pearcy, "Intertextuality and *La Damoiselle qui n'ot parler de foutre qu'i n'aust mal au cuer*," *Zeitschrift für romanische Philologie* 109 (1993): 526–38. Intertextual relationships, parodic or otherwise, between fabliaux and courtly texts are also studied by Nykrog, *Les Fabliaux*, 66–104, 227–30; Peter Dronke, *The Medieval Poet and His World* (Rome: Storia e Letteratura, 1984), 160–65; Albert Gier, "Chrétien de Troyes et les auteurs de fabliaux: La parodie du roman courtois," in *The Legacy of Chrétien de Troyes*, ed. Norris J. Lacy, Douglas Kelly, and Keith Busby, 2 vols. (Amsterdam: Rodopi, 1988), 2:207–14; Lacy, *Reading Fabliaux*, 46–59; and Anne Elizabeth Cobby, *Ambivalent Conventions: Formula and Parody in Old French* (Amsterdam: Rodopi, 1995), 23–54. Objections to the description of fabliaux in terms of "parody" or "burlesque" are raised by Ménard, *Les Fabliaux*, 206–12, and Dominique Boutet, *Les Fabliaux* (Paris: Presses Universitaires de France, 1985), 45–63.

37. Marie de France, *Guigemar*, in *Lais*, ed. Karl Warnke, trans. Laurence Harf-Lancner (Paris: Livre de Poche, 1990), vv. 533–34; Chrétien de Troyes, *Le Chevalier de la Charrette*, ed. and trans. Charles Méla (Paris: Livre de Poche, 1992), vv. 4681–82.

38. Donald Maddox, "Generic Intertextuality in Arthurian Literature: The Specular Encounter," in *Text and Intertext in Medieval Arthurian Literature*, ed. Norris J. Lacy (New York: Garland, 1996), 3 [3–24]; on the interpretation of fabliaux in manuscript context, see, among others, Keith Busby, *Codex and Context: Reading Old French Verse Narrative in Manuscript*, 2 vols. (Amsterdam: Rodopi, 2002), 1:437–63; Barbara Nolan, "Turning Over the Leaves of Medieval Fabliau-Anthologies: The Case of Bibliothèque Nationale MS. français 2173," *Medieval Perspectives* 8 (1998): 1–31; Barbara

Nolan, "Anthologizing Ribaldry: Five Anglo-Norman Fabliaux," in *Studies in the Harley Manuscript: The Scribes, Contents, and Social Contexts of British Library MS Harley 2253*, ed. Susanna Fein (Kalamazoo: Medieval Institute, 2000), 289–327; Tracy Adams, "The Cunningly Intelligent Characters of BNffr 19152," *MLN* 120, no. 4 (2005): 896–924; and Katherine A. Brown, *Boccaccio's Fabliaux: Medieval Short Stories and the Function of Reversal* (Gainesville: University Press of Florida, 2014).

39. The *D*-text further emphasizes that normal people, young and old, love saying "*foutre*," which is "a toz .i. mout doz mot" (a most pleasing word to everyone [D_D 27]). On the relationship between the language of "arrogance" and the construction of class in the fabliaux, see Kiril Petkov, "*Hom orgoilloz ne puet longues durer*: Mobility, Arrogance, and Class in the Old French Fabliaux," *Exemplaria* 18, no. 1 (2006): 137–74; cf. the discussion of "the conservatism of the fabliaux" in Lacy, *Reading Fabliaux*, 35–45.

40. This is even clearer in the *D*-text: the local men "se gaboient communement" (often joked together [D_D 37]) at the henpecked father's expense.

41. Crocker, "Disfiguring Gender," 348, 359.

42. Cf. the *D*-text's prefatory claim that its incipient story "n'est pas vilaine a dire, / mais moz por la gent faire rire" (is not uncouth to tell; it's just some words to make folk laugh [D_D 3–4]).

43. These characters are introduced in Guillaume de Lorris and Jean de Meun, *Le Roman de la Rose*, ed. Félix Lecoy, 3 vols. (Paris: Honoré Champion, 1973), vv. 2809–20. *Damoisele*'s anal *cornerre* is posted "por faire . . . honte et peor" (to inspire . . . shame and fear [*D* 157]) in thirsty "animals." However, the *cornerre* is also comparable to the guardian of the fountain in Chrétien de Troyes's *Le Chevalier au lion*; see Busby, "Courtly Literature," 80–81. As many critics have remarked, the issue of "proper" (in both senses) reference to sexual organs in genteel (women's) speech that is central to *Damoisele* (and *Escuiruel*) is debated by Amant and Raison, using the test case of the word *coilles*, in Jean de Meun's part of the *Rose* (vv. 6898–7174); earlier, Guillaume de Lorris's God of Love has forbidden the courtly Amant to "nomer vilainne chose" (name vulgar things [v. 2099]). See, among others, Nykrog, *Les Fabliaux*, 220–23; Muscatine, *Fabliaux*, 134–35, 146–50; Pearcy, "Modes of Signification," 163–64; Lacy, *Reading Fabliaux*, 79–81; and Bloch, "Modest Maids," 302–4.

44. The *damoisele* of the *ACE*-text arguably does even better, preempting her father's choice of a husband for her so as to select her own spouse based on criteria designed to ensure his sexual compatibility with her. Her swain would earn the approval of the early fourteenth-century canon lawyer William of Pagula, who holds, with Aquinas and Bonaventure, that women modestly prefer "to speak about sex in circumlocutions," and contends that husbands must therefore "be sensitive to their unspoken signs" and satisfy their sexual needs without making them avow their lust: James A. Brundage, *Law, Sex, and Christian Society in Medieval Europe* (Chicago: University of Chicago Press, 1987), 426–27.

45. Muñoz, *Disabusing Women*, 108–9.

46. *Porcelet*, in *NRCF*, 6:185–91, 343; *La Dame qui aveine demandoit pour Morel sa provende avoir*, in *NRCF*, 9:183–99, 305. Parenthetical references marked *M* give line numbers in the critical edition of *Morel*.

47. *La Sorisete des estopes*, in *NRCF*, 6:171–83, 340–42. *Sorisete* appears only in ms. Bern, Burgerbibliothek, 354, fols. 175ra-vb, 56ra-57ra. Parenthetical

references marked *S* give line numbers in the critical edition. An episode analogous to the *Sorisete* story features in Gautier le Leu's *Le Fol Vilain,* in *NRCF,* 9:149–68, 301–3 (see vv. 177–370 in the critical edition). The cognate narratives are compared by Pearcy, "Fabliau Intertextuality," 52–55, and *Logic and Humour,* 57–58.

48. This mother-in-law's instinctive collusion with her daughter to bamboozle a naïve bridegroom contrasts with another mother-in-law's move to secure her daughter's sexual satisfaction by exposing her own anatomy and explaining the mechanics of intercourse to the ignorant eponym of Gautier le Leu's *Le Sot Chevalier,* in *NRCF,* 5:313–35, 435–41 (see vv. 59–98 in the critical edition).

49. Gaunt, *Gender and Genre,* 266–67.

50. Burns, *Bodytalk,* 57. The woman's "mutilation in language, of language" also makes *Sorisete* a story about castration, according to Bloch, *Scandal,* 74–75. On semantics and deixis in the "Saussurean" *Sorisete,* see Ora Avni, *The Resistance of Reference: Linguistics, Philosophy, and the Literary Text* (Baltimore: Johns Hopkins University Press, 1990), 2–14.

51. Brundage, *Law, Sex, and Christian Society,* 471, 239. On the "marital debt" in medieval canon law, see also 198, 236–42, 278–88, 358–60.

52. Griffin, "Dirty Stories," 241.

53. Brundage, *Law, Sex, and Christian Society,* 247, 359–60.

54. Harris suggests, regarding a fifteenth-century Scottish pastourelle, that a young woman who offers her partner sexual instruction is framed as both "an ordinary peasant girl and a wise embodied vulva"—she refers to the "talking cunts" of *Le Chevalier qui fist parler les cons* (*NRCF,* 3:45–173, 412–29) and other Old French fabliaux, discussed by Burns, *Bodytalk,* 54–65—"teaching lessons about mutuality and negotiation to young men" (Harris, *Obscene Pedagogies,* 140). The same might be said of the woman in *Sorisete,* except that, in accordance with the fabliau's thematics of displacement, she speaks for the cunt (rather than vice versa) that is and is not "hers."

55. The couple's dialogue thus does not quite achieve the "tone of conjugal jocularity" in which spouses' sexual reconciliation is presented in Jehan Bodel's *Le Sohait des vez* (*The Fantasy of Cocks*): Perfetti, "The Lewd and the Ludic," 26–27; see *NRCF,* 6:259–72, 354–56. The outcome may, however, be an improvement even over the wife's somewhat exploitative relationship with the priest, whose courtly talk barely conceals a clear asymmetry in the lovers' status and power. Although the priest addresses the wife as "doce amie" (sweet beloved [*S* 13]), she calls him "sire" (my lord [*S* 17]) and (jokingly?) grants his request for a last roll in the hay because "je ne vos os escondire . . . que perdre ne voil vostre grace" (I don't dare to deny you . . . since I don't want to lose your favor [*S* 18–22]), and their liaison is described as predicated on his whims and pleasure: "li prestes son boen en faisoit, / qant il voloit et li plaisoit" (the priest had his way with her / whenever he wanted, as it pleased him [*S* 9–10]).

56. Stefanie Goyette, "Fabricating Monstrosity: Secrets and Violence in the *Lay of Graelent* and Several Old French Fabliaux," *Preternature* 6, no. 2 (2017): 231 [212–35].

57. Crocker, "Disfiguring Gender," 342–43; see also Gaunt, *Gender and Genre,* 274, and William Burgwinkle, "The Marital and the Sexual," in *The Cambridge Companion to Medieval French Literature,* ed. Simon Gaunt and Sarah Kay (Cambridge: Cambridge University Press, 2008), 233 [225–37]. The

husband in *Morel*, for instance, becomes a figure of fun precisely for being too solicitous of his wife's sexual pleasure and consent; he invents the euphemism of "Blackie's oats" so that his wife can ask for sex when, and only when, she wants it, because when she is under the weather, he tells her, "je n'ose a toi gesir / pour acomplir nostre desir, / car je trop correciez seroie, / se mal ou anui te faisoie" (I do not dare to lie with you to consummate our desire, for I would be too upset if I caused you any harm or displeasure [*M* 69–72]).

58. Crocker, "Disfiguring Gender," 346, 354.

Texas Tech University
lucas.wood@ttu.edu

Revisiting Potiphar's Wife

A European Perspective on a Character in Early Modern Drama

DINAH WOUTERS

Abstract

This article offers a diachronic and European overview of the developments and changes in the dramatic characterization of Potiphar's wife, who is an exceptional female character in early modern drama. The first part focuses on three humanist authors writing in three different languages: Pandolfo Collenuccio in Italian, Miguel de Carvajal in Spanish, and Cornelius Crocus in Latin. The second part changes the scope and the method of the investigation by tracing the different approaches among circa sixty dramas over the course of two centuries. The article distinguishes seven groups of responses to and departures from the humanists' early treatment of the character: the group of authors, mostly writing in Latin and German, who follow the Dutch humanists; the plays in which the character is merely functional; the plays in which she is a tragic character, either within a comedy or a tragedy; the group of mostly Protestant plays that vilify her; Spanish drama, which makes her a romance character; and Jesuit drama, which leaves her out of the action.

The story of the failed seduction of the patriarch Joseph by his master Potiphar's wife and her false accusation of rape against him is considered a part of world literature,[1] both in this specific version from the book of Genesis,[2] and as an instance of the literary archetype of the married woman who falls in love with her stepson or her servant.[3] The story of Joseph is also one of the most beloved themes of early modern drama, where Potiphar's wife is a rather unusual character. Most of the female characters that appear in biblical drama are the exact opposite of Potiphar's wife: they are chaste women such as Esther, Susanna, or early Christian martyrs. Religious drama, moreover, hardly treats the themes of love and passion. About a century ago, Raymond Lebegue remarked that in French religious tragedy, "l'amour ne joue aucun rôle: aussi n'y

Medievalia et Humanistica, New Series, Number 47 (Reinhold F. Glei and Maik Goth, eds.), Rowman & Littlefield, 2022.

trouve-t-on aucune réplique des figures les plus originales et les plus attachantes du théâtre de Sénèque: Phèdre et Médée."[4] Potiphar's wife is an exception. She is sensual and unfaithful, driven by sexual desire and amorous passion. She can be both tragic and comic, both elevated and vulgar. At the same time, she is one of the main characters in a biblical story that school plays utilize to teach the virtue of chastity.

Jean Lebeau and Ruprecht Wimmer have made extensive studies of Joseph drama in the German countries.[5] The former included a chapter about the wife of Potiphar in these dramas between 1533 and 1625.[6] But how does the image sketched by Lebeau change when we include drama from other regions as well? The situation that Lebeau describes for the German lands until the first quarter of the seventeenth century is marked by a strong coherence in how plays represent Potiphar's wife. The characterization by the Dutch humanists, especially Crocus, is dominant, although her complexity and importance is reduced and eventually transformed into a misogynist stereotype. I want to investigate whether this coherence holds up if we apply a more transnational approach, by including different regions and different languages.[7] Did the character as created by Crocus travel beyond this cultural sphere, or did other humanist models exert their influence? I want to approach the character from a European perspective, over the course of two centuries. I will only summarily provide information about the authors of the plays that I discuss, with the exception of three early humanist plays. My focus will be on giving an overview of the changing roles of this character through different decades, literary trends, and languages. I will sketch the relations within and between the groups that I distinguish in broad outlines.

In the first part of this article, I want to focus on the three humanist authors who have laid the foundation for a more elaborate and complex approach to the character. They have done so in three different languages: Pandolfo Collenuccio in Italian, Miguel de Carvajal in Spanish, and Cornelius Crocus in Latin. Collenuccio's play was first performed in 1504 in Ferrara, although it was printed only in 1523 in Venice; the publication of the plays by the Spaniard Carvajal and the Dutchman Crocus followed in 1535 and 1536, respectively. In the second part, I change the scope and the method of my investigation by tracing the different approaches among circa sixty dramas over the course of two centuries. I distinguish seven groups of responses to and departures from the humanists' early treatment of the character. In this way, I want to offer a diachronic and European overview of the developments and changes in the characterization of this one exceptional female character.

Collenuccio

Pandolfo Collenuccio (1444–1504) was a humanist and ambassador in the service of Lorenzo il Magnifico and Ercole I d'Este.[8] He wrote his *Comedia di Iacob e Ioseph* in Ferrara at the end of his life. Since the early seventies of the sixteenth century, the Ferrara of Duke Ercole had become the capital of theatrical experimentation, especially with regard to the revival of Roman comedy.[9] In 1486, during the carnival festivities, an Italian translation of Plautus's *Menaechmi* was performed before thousands of people. This may have been "the first presentation of a Roman comedy in translation anywhere in Europe."[10] A year later, Carnival featured another Plautus play, *Amphitruo*, this time in a translation by Collenuccio himself.[11]

Collenuccio's *Comedia di Iacob e Ioseph* closely follows the Bible: in six acts, the play tells the whole story of Joseph, from receiving a coat by his father to Jacob's move to Egypt.[12] The play is sometimes considered a *sacra rappresentazione*, identifying it with the ecclesiastical drama that was created in Florence around the middle of the fifteenth century.[13] Like many of the Florentine plays, Collenuccio chooses an Old Testament story that carries a message about good leadership and civic virtues.

Elisa Curti, however, notes some important differences between the Tuscan *rappresentazioni* and the comedy from Ferrara.[14] First, Collenuccio does not use the *ottava rima*, characteristic of the *rappresentazione*, but a *terzina*, a meter characteristic of didactic literature. Second, Curti finds little common ground between Collenuccio's play and two contemporary *rappresentazioni* about Joseph. Among other differences, the *Comedia* eschews the use of captions and comic additions. In contrast, Collenuccio's play heavily stresses the moral themes of the story, such as Stoic patience in the face of *iniuria* and the destructiveness of *invidia* that is also central to Seneca's dramas.[15] These themes are expressed through long reflexive monologues.

Curti concludes that the *Comedia*, as a humanist Old Testament play written in Italian, forms something of a *unicum*:

[I]l testo del Collenuccio, carico della sua sentenziosa esemplarità, rappresenta un esperimento significativo di dramma sacro di impronta umanistica, non assimilabile né alle sacre rappresentazioni fiorentine, che pure gli erano note e da cui trae il tema veterotestamentario, né alla tradizione delle messe in scena religiose del nord. La Comedia pare ricercare nuove espressioni per il teatro religioso, più classicheggianti e "regolari" [. . .][16]

It is good to note, however, that the *sacra rappresentazioni*, too, did not stem from a popular milieu but from a humanistic one: Florentine intellectuals invented the genre as an "innovative and cutting-edge tool for the civic and religious education of new generations of citizens in Medicean Florence."[17] Thus, we could consider Collenuccio's play as an experiment in trying to implement a similar educational program in Ferrara, by adopting the concept rather than the specific forms of the Florentine tradition.

The episode in Potiphar's house is not of central importance in Collenuccio's play. It takes up slightly more than half of the third act. The act opens with a monologue by Potiphar's servant Sesostris, who complains that of the many people who have power over him in the household, some are haughty and overambitious, others avaricious and unjust. There is one, however, to whom Sesostris looks up and whom he is willing to obey at the slightest hint, namely Joseph. At that, Potiphar's wife, here called Beronica, enters and also begins praising Joseph to her servant Sydonia. She talks about his beauty and noble manners, and confesses her passion for the young man. She asks Sydonia for advice, who tells her to banish these feelings from her heart. Clearly, this is not the advice that Beronica had hoped to hear. Rather, she wants to hear from her servant by what means she should attempt to fulfill her desire. As in Euripides's and Seneca's *Phaedra*, although after a much shorter exchange, Sydonia gives in. She advises her mistress to be persistent with Joseph and, above all, to make sure that nobody finds out.

Next, Beronica hurries to Joseph. In contrast to the *rappresentazioni* and French mystery plays, this is not the first time Beronica talks to Joseph. She refers to the many times that she has told him about her love for him ("Iosep io te ho pregato tante volte"). Joseph answers with the words he speaks in the Bible: Potiphar has entrusted to him everything in the house except his wife, and he will not betray that trust. Joseph speaks about honor, Beronica about love. She asks one last time for him to love her as she loves him, and then hurriedly leaves because she is afraid that someone will notice them:

Non e tempo star qui, ma sii pregato
Isep; amar tu me, come anchio te amo
Ti lasso, emene vo col cor piagato.[18]

Joseph then calls on God to take away these wicked thoughts from Beronica, saying that he would rather die than commit such a crime as she asks of him. Sydonia has witnessed the whole scene from afar and worries about the reaction of her mistress.[19] In a monologue, she sketches a psychological portrait of Beronica as a woman wholly and madly consumed by passion, similar to Phaedra: she talks about her "furor" and "ira," says she is "going mad" ("impazir"), calls her "rabbiosa" and "furiosa" but also "donna superba, altiera, insidiosa." She compares her to both a snake and a tiger:

Che se lo amore in odio convertisce
Serpe non fia di lei piu venenosa
[. . .]
Se durerà di fargli pur contrasto
Come Tigre affamata che non trova,
Pei piccol figiolin, ne per se pasto.[20]

Whereas in the earlier scenes, Beronica seemed more pitiful than dangerous, now a feeling of impending doom creeps into the play. In the next scene, the worst has already happened. This is the scene where Joseph flees from his chamber while recounting what took place there:

Io mi ero posto nel mio albergo solo
Per riueder mei conti e mie ragione
Ecco che me assalto, quasi in vn volo
Questa fera impudica, e si mi pone
Le mani adosso senza alcun risguardo
Pur per sforzar mia casta oppinione.[21]

Following this scene, we watch Beronica utter her false accusation. In her version of the story, Joseph came to her room to assault her. After a monologue by Potiphar, the scene turns to the prison to which Joseph is led.

In Collenuccio's comedy, although Beronica does not yet play a large role, she is no longer just the one-dimensional figure that she is in the *rappresentazioni*. The difference is due not so much to the words that she speaks as to the characterization of her by Sydonia. Dramatic tension is derived from the fact that the reader or spectator never sees Beronica at her worst. We must believe Sydonia and Joseph that she really is as deranged and maniacal as they say. Unlike in the *rappresentazioni* and mystery plays, Beronica does not explicitly and straightforwardly ask Joseph to sleep with her. She only talks about love, until the moment when she assaults him. This uncertainty and duplicity incites fear and plays into stereotypes of the irrational woman whose love can easily turn to hate.

The depiction of Beronica reflects the influence of Seneca on humanist drama. Sydonia's speech assembles all the keywords, such as "furor" and "rabiosa." Her comparison of Beronica to wild animals finds a parallel in Seneca's description of people in the grip of anger. In his work *De Ira*, he describes anger as an inhumane and dehumanizing state, brought on by animal instinct.[22] Beronica is a good example of the type that Vincent Dupuis calls "la furieuse," namely a female character driven by spectacular and wild passion.[23] On the one hand, it is typical of humanist drama to pay more attention to the depiction of the affective state of a character than the actions that produce that state. On the other hand, Vincent Dupuis points out that the figure of the *furieuse* is particularly central to sixteenth-century drama. Speaking about French drama of this period, he says:

Il est significatif que les premières figures centrales du théâtre français soient des furieuses. La tragédie humaniste, bien que de facture érudite, reconduit une peur ancestrale, populaire, qui remonte aux souches de la société patriarcale, mais qui prend dans le cadre des procès de sorcellerie une ampleur sans précédent: la peur de la femme.[24]

Carvajal

Like Collenuccio's play, *Carvajal's Tragedia llamada Josefina* is a unique blend of classicizing and popularizing tendencies. Melveena McKendrick notes that it is "unique in that it is a five-act play on a religious theme written for public performance and shows all the unconcern for unity of time and place of the popular religious drama."[25] Carvajal's tragedy has been lauded as one of the prime achievements of Spanish sixteenth-century drama. It was written in a transitional period, before the standardization of the type of allegorical play known as *auto sacramental.*[26] In contrast to the one-act *auto*, Carvajal's play is a five-act tragedy in the Senecan style, with prologues and choruses respectively at the beginning and at the end of each act.

Its first print edition is lost but is recorded to have been published in 1535.[27] Sources about the early years of the author are equally scant, and it is not clear when and where Carvajal received his humanist education. We know that he came from an illustrious family in the cathedral city of Plasencia, in the Spanish region Extremadura. If the play was first published in 1535, then a good guess would be to say that it was first performed in Plasencia at the feast of Corpus Christi somewhere in the early years of the 1530s.

The play uses not only the biblical story and patristic exegesis, as in the case of Collenuccio and Crocus, but also Jewish exegesis and folklore material. This, among other things, has led to speculation that Carvajal was a *converso*. Even if he himself did not come from a formerly Jewish family, Plasencia had a large *converso* community, and the prologue to the *Tragedia Josephina* alludes to this fact. Scholarship around Carvajal has focused on this Jewish element and whether it reflects anti-Semitism or not.[28]

Similarly to Collenuccio's play, but to a much higher degree, Carvajal develops the character of Potiphar's wife into the first "woman of flesh and blood" in Spanish drama.[29] The episode where Joseph is a slave at Potiphar's house and is in prison takes up the second act of the play. Whereas Collenuccio and Crocus show the seduction as one encounter and hint at previous attempts, Carvajal uses three scenes to build up to the assault.

In the first scene, their conversation remains implicit. Zenobia (as she is called here) calls Joseph to her room but has nothing to tell him. When he asks permission to leave, she takes this as a personal insult and gets angry with him for no apparent reason. Left alone, Zenobia bemoans her obsession with Joseph. At this point, there is still some doubt in her as to whether she should give in to her desire. She mainly seems angry and ashamed at herself. She says:

¿Cómo puede aquesto ser,
Que siendo yo tal señora,
Y en quien mi marido adora
Con extremado querer,
Me deje yo así vencer
De un muchacho, y extranjero,
Mi esclavo y mi prisionero!
Yo no lo puedo creer.[30]

Zenobia is horrified to think of the damage it would do to her reputation if the ladies of the court would find out about her affair with a servant. She manages, however, to convince herself that she just cannot help it, and then she begins to worry about how she will convince Joseph:

Ay que no se que me haga
si le hable si le dexe
si le acuse si le aquexe
por dar remedio a mi llaga[31]

In the last part of her long monologue, she throws all caution to the wind and hardens in her resolve. She decides to force herself ("Quierome agora esforçar") to force Joseph ("si le fuerço"), and if her husband finds out, to tell him that it was Joseph who forced her ("dire que me es esforçador").[32]

In contrast to the distance between the audience and the character in Collenuccio's play, Carvajal gives us access to Zenobia's mind, showing how she is not simply the victim of an overpowering passion but how she deludes herself into thinking that she is. She tells herself that she cannot fight her urges, but this pose is contradicted by the fact that she plans everything beforehand. She plans the seduction, she plans to use force if Joseph does not give in, and she plans to accuse him of rape if they are caught.

The editor of the play, Joseph Gillet, has shown that there are certain similarities between the *Tragedia Josephina* and the French mystery play *Le mistère du vieil testament*, which was printed in Paris first around 1500 and again twenty years later.[33] Because most of the similarities he finds seem to derive from Jewish sources, he concedes that there is no necessary direct link. I want to point out, however, some more convergences between Carvajal and the French mystery plays, particularly in the seduction scenes. For instance, the *Mistère du vieil testament* is the first drama that we know of that gives a monologue to Potiphar's wife, and although it is short, its contents are similar to Zenobia's monologue. "La Dame" considers in what way she could best persuade Joseph,[34] expresses her fear that Joseph would tell on her and she would lose her honor ("Et, on le sçait, je suis infame."), is amazed and ashamed of herself ("je suis esbahye, je considère ma follye"), but concludes that she is forced by love and is not to blame ("Mais, bref, amour me contrainct tant / Qu'il sera force que je prie / Joseph pour estre mon amant").[35] We find here Zenobia's monologue in miniature, minus the resolve to accuse him of rape if something goes wrong.

In the second confrontation between them, things are open on the table, but although Zenobia has uttered her threat in an indirect way, she is not yet openly threatening Joseph. At this point, she still tries to convince him by offering him freedom and wealth.[36] Potiphar arrives just in time to prevent the situation from escalating any further. The escalation comes after Potiphar has left for a feast at court. From here on, Zenobia is described as maniacally focused on having her desire fulfilled and, if it cannot be fulfilled, taking revenge. Discarding her earlier sense of pride, she now humiliates herself before Joseph, saying:

no menosprecies ansi
a mi que soy tu señora
tratasme como vna mora
llegate aca ya boçal
haz cuenta que soy tu ygual
y aun que soy tu seruidora.[37]

Faced with Zenobia's crude words, threats, and insults, Joseph speaks of his pity for her, an element that we will also encounter in Crocus's Latin play.[38] But his empathy only fans her anger. Even after she has grabbed Joseph's mantle and called out for her husband to come, she asks Joseph twice to reconsider, but calls for his death when he refuses:

abraçame y no aya mas
no quieres pues moriras[39]

Joseph Gillet has given a wonderful description of the subtlety and complexity of this character:

> Though it is clear that she has only fear and contempt for Potiphar, she is no wanton. Strong barriers of personal pride and regard for public opinion must break before confusion overwhelms her. Religion to her means little; possible destruction is readily accepted, and the elemental woman rapidly emerges, single-minded, but far from simple; angry or wheedling, threatening, reasoning, in shifting moods of contempt and possessive pride, tired impatience and self-abasement, culminating in a trembling and desperate surrender.[40]

Gillet suggested that Zenobia is modeled on the classical Phaedra. In his opinion, Zenobia is driven "by a power beyond her resistance," which humanizes her lust and ennobles her suffering.[41] It is telling for the complexity of the character that I am unable to agree fully with him on this point. I see in Zenobia a combination of the languishing and *furor*-driven character of Phaedra and the practical, plotting character from the mystery plays. Rather than reading her monologue as the desperate attempt to preserve honor and ethics, I read it as a self-delusional speech that uses the rhetoric of higher power to justify cruelty. But the delusion is exposed by the fact that Zenobia plans her every move beforehand, unlike in the mystery plays. Although opinions might differ on how far Zenobia can be held accountable, however, there is no doubt that she is one of the most complex and layered female characters in sixteenth-century drama.

Crocus

Born around 1500 in Amsterdam, Cornelius Crocus studied in Leuven and returned to Amsterdam to become rector of one of the municipal schools.[42] He was a Catholic priest and joined the Jesuit order in 1550, during the last year of his life. He defended Catholic doctrine in his theological works and reached a certain fame as a theologian.

In contrast to the plays by Collenuccio and Carvajal, Crocus's *Comoedia sacra* does not take classical tragedy, but comedy, as its model. Crocus was undoubtedly influenced by the many performances of Roman dramas in Leuven.[43] Crocus adopts the language, style, and some of the characters of Plautus and Terence, but replaces the story and the questionable morals with a biblical tale and a Christian hero.

One of the most remarkable innovations of this play is that it focuses exclusively on the period between Joseph's arrival at Potiphar's house and his liberation from prison, leaving out the conflict between him and his brothers. This does not mean that the whole plot revolves around the attempted seduction, however. The confrontation between Joseph and Potiphar's wife, here called Sephirach, is still a single scene and not three, as in Carvajal's play. Acts 2, 3, and the beginning of 4 show the predicament of Potiphar, who must choose whether to believe his wife or his trusted overseer. For the first time, Potiphar is given more than a merely functional role. Finally, the fifth act celebrates the triumph of Joseph's willpower and chastity, when he is led out of prison on his way to a glorious future.

The play starts with a slave speech, as was the case in Collenuccio. The slave monologue is also a standard scene in classical comedy, however. The slave Mago complains about the injustice of slavery and the inconsiderateness of masters. Instead of holding a paean on Joseph (as Sesostris does in Collenuccio's play), Mago complains of Sephirach, who has been irascible and unbearable since Joseph joined the household. At that moment, Sephirach herself finds him outside and heaps abuse on him.

Next follows Sephirach's monologue. In contrast to Carvajal's Zenobia, Sephirach is not ashamed that she is in love with Joseph: she says that his beauty and virtue make him worthy of such a love, even though he is a slave. She does find him ungrateful toward her, and reasons that every other slave would consider it an honor to have his mistress at his feet ("[. . .] heram habere supplicem sibi suam?"). She convinces herself that there is still some hope and goes for the soft approach ("Aggrediar blande, ac benedice, spero emollescet."). This includes throwing a last look in the mirror to check her appearance:

Sic culta incedo? Satin' haec me uestis decet? dedi equidem
Operam sedulo. Ita poliendo atque ornando hunc contriui diem.[44]

Sephirach intercepts Joseph and loses no time in revealing her intentions, greeting him with the words: "Joseph mi, maxume / Animo exoptate meo, mea uita, mea uoluptas unica."[45] At that, Joseph groans: "Ecce autem iterum."[46] Now follows a very long exchange between the two, coated in the love-language of Ovid and Terence.[47] Two things in this conversation are markedly different from the dramas by Collenuccio and Carvajal. First, as his response to Sephirach's greeting indicates, Joseph does not have endless patience but shows irritation: he says that her words fill him with disgust and complains that he is hearing all this for the hundredth time. Second, as the conversation goes on, Sephirach turns from blandishments to arguments. This serves a didactic goal: every argument that Sephirach makes to convince Joseph gives him the chance not only to show his steadfastness but also to explain why he should not give in.

When Sephirach argues that he should profit from his youth and his beauty, Joseph counters that youth and beauty are perishable, in opposition to the true beauty of virtue. Similarly, when she says that he has no right to reject her because she owns him, he answers that his slavery is of the body and not of the mind. When she argues that adultery is a sin shared by many people, he responds that it is a sin nonetheless, and that they both have their duty toward Potiphar. She says that there is no chance that they will be found out; he counters that a righteous person does not sin even if it remains hidden. She asks for only a kiss, he refuses to give in because it would lead to further things. Last, she exclaims that it is stupid to refuse something good that is given without a charge. Joseph denies that what is given is good. Sephirach now loses her patience, and her love turns to hate. She exchanges her arguments for threats, but Joseph refuses to back down. As in Carvajal's version, this is the moment where Joseph expresses his empathy for Sephirach by saying that he feels sorry for her. This expression of pity does finally activate a feeling of wounded pride: "Ten' me irridere inultum seruom hominem sinam? / Mortuam me malim."[48] She storms out of the room with the words "Tu uideris, scelus."[49]

The act ends with a worried monologue by Joseph, and the next act begins with Joseph again, who is now fleeing after the assault. A third difference with the previous two dramas comes to the fore in the third and four acts. Whereas in all of the previous dramatic versions, Potiphar merely gets angry and sends Joseph to prison, here the conflict between Sephirach and Joseph is extended to Potiphar. Coming home, Potiphar finds Joseph in distress and asks him what is wrong. Joseph foregoes the chance to tell his version of the story first, supposedly both because he still hopes that Sephirach will not accuse him and because he is afraid that Potiphar will not believe him. When Sephirach does accuse him, Joseph is present to defend himself, which he only does halfheartedly out of a sense of propriety. Potiphar, impressed by the calm demeanor of his servant, begins to doubt his wife. Sephirach rages and wants Joseph executed, but Potiphar refuses. After sending her away, he asks Joseph whether he is guilty. Joseph remains silent, however.[50] When Potiphar asks why, Joseph answers: "Quia me eloqui indignum est, here."[51] At that, Potiphar has no choice but to send him to prison. In a monologue, however, he expresses his regret and his doubts about the truth of the situation, adding his hope that he might release Joseph from prison when the dust has settled. Crocus, therefore, does not only add depth to the character of Sephirach but also to that of her husband.

In fact, the focus on Sephirach's feelings is somewhat weakened by the fact that she serves as a comic character. Sephirach speaks like a Terentian courtesan, and the irritation that she causes Mago and Joseph is used to comic effect. Therefore, although she is a much richer character than she is in the mystery plays, she lacks the tragic dimension of Collenuccio's Beronica and the emotional depth of Carvajal's Zenobia. The actual conflict is shifted onto Joseph and Potiphar. The struggle for Joseph is not about resisting Sephirach's seductions (they only cause him loathing), but about defending himself without causing dishonor upon Potiphar by exposing his wife. He chooses to remain silent so that Potiphar can continue to hold his head high. Potiphar, from his side, is torn between loyalty to his wife and trust in a servant whom he loved as a son.

Summing up, these three earliest humanist dramatic adaptations of the story give us not only three different names for but also three quite different versions of the character of Potiphar's wife. The Italian play paints her as a Senecan *furieuse*, a wild woman whose incontrollable passion turns to hate in an instant. In the Spanish play, Zenobia is still partly the scheming wife from the mystery plays, which means that she carries more responsibility for her deeds than Beronica. She seems capable of controlling her *furor*, but chooses to use it as an excuse. Finally, in the Latin comedy, amorous *furor* is not only not an excuse but is also a ridiculous posture with serious consequences. Collenuccio still clings closely to his classical model, which was in itself a daring innovation in the treatment of an Old Testament theme. Carvajal and Crocus each thoroughly Christianize their classical model, the Spaniard by undermining the tragic pose of the *furieuse*, and the Dutchman by contrasting comic libidinous language with its less comic consequences.

Editions and Reprints

Each of these plays was successful enough to be reprinted a few times, but to differing degrees. Collenuccio's tragedy, as we have seen, was first reprinted nineteen years after its initial performance in Ferrara. Then, between 1523 and 1564, the play went through eight editions in Venice with various printers.[52] Carvajal's play is preserved in three copies that reflect three different editions. After the first edition of 1535 in Salamanca, which is lost, the text was printed in 1540 in Palencia, in 1545 in Sevilla, and one year later in Toledo.[53] It appears that later reprints might have been limited by the inquisition. In the Index of Valladolid from 1559 there appears a play called *Farsa llamada Josefina*, and, again in 1599, the Inquisition denies an appeal by the city of Plasencia to stage a *Comedia llamada Josefina*, apparently the same text.[54] The reason is that the play depicts the scene where Joseph explains dreams in prison, which could encourage popular beliefs in dream divination, and the scene where Potiphar's wife tries to seduce Joseph. We are not certain whether this *farsa/comedia* is the same or a related text to Carvajal's *tragedia*, but the fact that the appeal for its performance in 1599 comes from Plasencia makes it very probable.

Although indicative of a wide readership, the reprints of the Italian and the Spanish play pale in comparison to the number of times the Latin play was reprinted. Although it was the only drama written by the author, Crocus's play became one of the most popular Latin school dramas. This is reflected in its publishing history, not only in numbers but also in the variety of cities where it appeared. First printed in 1536 in Antwerp, it reached Cologne, Paris, and Strasbourg in 1537; Augsburg in 1539; Basel in 1540; and Dortmund in 1549. In all of these places, it was printed more than once. Even in 1613, Antwerp was still printing Crocus's *Josephus*. In Basel in 1541 and then again in 1547, two publishers included Crocus's play in their anthologies of sacred drama.[55] Whereas the publication of Collenuccio's play traveled from Ferrara to Venice, and Carvajal's play circulated throughout Castile and Aragon but not beyond, Crocus's Latin play traveled at least the extent of the Rhine, as far as we can deduct from known publications.

After the Pioneers

I have discussed these three humanist pioneers in detail. In the second half of this article, I want to give an overview in broad lines of what happens to Potiphar's wife afterward. This overview will necessarily exclude a close reading of the texts. In general, the characterization of Potiphar's wife rarely reaches the same complexity as it does in Carvajal and Crocus, although there are some significant exceptions.

Followers of Crocus

Humanist comedy, and especially sacred comedy, turned out to be an excellent didactic tool: it teaches good Latin and good morals at the same time, in an engaging format and with a touch of humor.[56] Pupils read and discussed these texts in class together with their teacher and then brought them to the stage themselves. This practical use of dramatic texts explains why Crocus's drama could spread so widely and have such a long-lasting impact. However, as Jean Lebeau and Ruprecht Wimmer pointed out, his impact on later plays did not mean that these plays adopted his structural innovations.[57] The most daring aspect of his play, the omission of the larger biblical story, was rarely followed. When it occurs, it is in tragedies that take their cue from the tragedy of *Phaedra*, not from comedy.

There are two exceptions. The first is the play by Crocus's fellow Dutch humanist Georgius Macropedius, which was first published in 1544. Macropedius's *fabula sacra* elaborates Joseph's relationship with the people in Potiphar's household. In this version, the prefigurative dimension of Joseph as Christ is quite strong. Not only does Joseph withstand Aegla's (Potiphar's wife's) seduction, he converts half of the household to Christianity, including the daughter of the house. The character of Aegla develops in a different direction and gains more maturity and realism. She is depicted as the neglected wife of a husband who is often absent. Uniquely in all of the Joseph dramas from the sixteenth century, the character sincerely repents and receives forgiveness. Although Macropedius makes abundant use of the structure and dialogues of Crocus's comedy, his own play is different in a way that foreshadows a trend of a few decades later, namely, a preference for realism and novelistic narrative extensions.[58]

The second exception is the *Josephiados Comoedia* by Ondrej Rochotsky, or Rochotius, a Slovak humanist and schoolteacher working in Bohemia.[59] Rochotius's comedy reads like a combination of Crocus and Macropedius, with some additions and a long fifth act that betray the same tendency for narrative enlargement that we saw in Macropedius's play.[60] But before we come to that development, let me summarize what Lebeau has said about Crocus's influence on Netherlandish and German dramatists with respect to the character of Potiphar's wife.

All Joseph plays written after 1536 in this cultural area characterized by German and Dutch humanism clearly show the influence of Crocus's and Macropedius's plays. The Latin plays do so to a larger degree than the German ones. These Latin Joseph plays were written by the southern German schoolteachers Andreas Diether and Martinus Balticus, the Lutheran professor of theology Aegidius Hunnius, the Catholic rector of the Haarlem gymnasium Cornelius Schonaeus, and the German Lutheran pastor and schoolmaster Theodorus Rhodius. Despite their fondness for Crocus, the role of Potiphar's wife becomes less prominent in these plays. The reason is that they do not adopt the innovative narrative structures of Crocus and Macropedius. Although we recognize Crocus and Macropedius in the rhetoric of the monologues and dialogues, sometimes even verbatim (as in the play by Andreas Diether), these later authors return to the full story of Joseph, in which the episode at Potiphar's house is just one incident.

The same is true for the German plays, which make Potiphar into the type of a bourgeois merchant and which subject Potiphar's wife to a stricter morality. The Augsburg rector Xystus Betuleius, for instance, makes his seduction scene much shorter. In the prologue to his Latin *Susanna* (1537), written in the time between the first performance and the publication of his Joseph play, he lashes out at Crocus's Sephirach. Criticizing the view that the genre of sacred comedy contains fewer immoral characters than Terence's plays, as Crocus suggests in his prologue to Joseph, Betuleius calls Crocus's Sephirach "a shameless and reprobate whore" who does not know her equal among Terence's prostitutes.[61]

Further, the Swiss dramatist Hans von Rüte translates Crocus's play and inserts it almost in its entirety into his own *Hystoria*, which tells Joseph's story from beginning to end. He adds a few scenes, however, where Potiphar chides his wife and even takes her to court. In contrast to Macropedius's play, therefore, the seductress does not receive forgiveness but punishment. The same moralizing streak of misogyny occurs in Jacob Ruf's Swiss play from 1540, where Potiphar is inclined to excuse Joseph's alleged crime because of the "huerisch gmuet" ("whorish nature") of women like his wife.[62]

Crocus's and Macropedius's impact is also felt in four plays that are not written in German or Latin, but in Polish, Spanish, and Dutch. First, a play that follows Crocus very explicitly is the Polish *Żywot Józefa z pokolenia żydowskiego, syna Jakubowego* (*The Life of Joseph of the Tribe of the Jews, the Son of Jacob*) by the Polish author Mikołaj Rey, published in 1545. The third act clearly leans on Crocus and Macropedius, and Rej adopts a few characters' names from Crocus as well.[63]

Second, there is a Spanish comedy by Lope de Vega (1629/1630).[64] Contrary to other Spanish plays, which I will discuss presently, Lope's play still leans quite closely on Carvajal's version and the biblical story, instead of focusing on Joseph's romance and marriage with Aseneth. Lope also seems to have taken inspiration from the Dutch humanists. Aseneth is not a character in his play. Instead, the play has a double focus: on the one hand, Lope draws a parallel between the betrayal and reconciliation between Joseph, his brothers, and Jacob, and on the other, between Joseph, Potiphar's wife Nicela and Potiphar. The scene opens with a seduction attempt by Nicela, who asks Joseph to tell her his story. In one of the last scenes, just before his father arrives, Joseph forgives Nicela and does her the favor of promoting Potiphar. The only earlier play that has this reconciliation scene is the one by Macropedius.

Last, the model of Crocus is still felt in two Dutch plays. The first was published in 1639 by the obscure author Jan Tonnis from Emden, who might have been connected to Chambers of Rhetoric. Tonnis's fourth act is made to encompass the scope of Crocus's play and contains many reminiscences, not the least of which is the name Syphora. "Sephora" is also the name of the character in the 1662 play *De historie van den suyveren Patriarch Joseph* (*The History of the Chaste Patriarch Joseph*) by the cleric Willem Zeebots, although this play, written for his small parish in Brabant, is more vulgar than the one by Tonnis.[65] Zeebots uses the character of Potiphar's wife to bring a misogynist moral: "Daer'n is geen meerder pest, dan eene quade vrou. / Geen duvel in de hel kan meerder quaet bedryven, / En d'meeste dat hy doet dat doet hy door de wyven."[66]

Functional Role

Before Crocus left his mark on the Joseph theme in 1536, the role of Potiphar's wife was just a functional one. This is the case in the Rhetoroman *La Historia da Joseph* by the Swiss reformer Jean Travers, which was first performed in 1530,[67] and in Joachim Greff's German "Spil," written for the gymnasium of Magdeburg in 1534.[68]

In a handful of German, mostly Lutheran, plays, the reduction of the role to a purely functional one seems a deliberate undoing of the character's importance, as these plays do adopt various elements from other humanist dramas. We see this reduction of the role in the plays by the Cologne printer Peter Jordan (1540), the Austrian schoolteacher Thomas Brunner (1566), and the schoolteacher Bartholomaeus Leschke (1571), who taught at Lubań in Upper Lusetia. Jean Lebeau notes that in these dramas, religious rigor and moralistic zeal repress the rhetorical creativity and exuberance found in other Joseph plays of the time.[69]

Two later plays that are linguistically isolated from the rest of the corpus adhere loyally to the biblical story. This is the case in the Swedish *Josephi Historia* by Thomas Gevaliensis (1601)[70] and in the English *Seventh Pageant of Joseph*, from the Catholic *Stonyhurst Pageants* (1610–1642).[71] Last, there is a geographically isolated play that treats the character in the same succinct manner, although it adds allegorical personifications:

the *auto historial* by the Mexican writer Sor Juana Inés de la Cruz, written in 1692.[72] *El Cetro de José* has two short scenes in which Joseph runs away from Potiphar's wife, and she is incited by the personifications Inteligencia, Envidia, and Lucero.

A Tragic Character in a Comic World

Some dramatists stress the tragic potential of the character, even when they do not make their play into a tragedy, and even though Potiphar's wife is just one of the characters with whom Joseph comes into conflict. This is the same model as the one used by Collenuccio and Carvajal.

First, the 1540 comedy by Thiebold Gart, mayor of Schlettstadt (Sélestat), is an exception within its German humanist setting in several ways.[73] One reason is that it explicitly incorporates figurative exegesis, in the form of commentary by Jesus and the prophets, who appear as characters. However, the second act, which includes everything that happens in Potiphar's house, lacks an exegesis. Instead, Gart composes two monologues for Sophora that heavily make use of Ovidian language in order to elevate her character to a tragic grandeur. Joseph, in fact, does not speak many words in Gart's version of the seduction. Jean Lebeau says: "Pour la première fois, dans nos comédies, l'épouse de Potiphar ne nous apparaît pas sous les dehors d'une vulgaire courtisane, d'une femme dépravée ou d'une brave bourgeoise troublée par son beau domestique. C'est une héroïne de tragédie qui parle ici."[74] Of course, if we look at it from a European context, both Collenuccio and Carvajal had done this before.

Second, there is the French *Joseph le Chaste* by the Parisian priest Nicolas de Montreux (1601).[75] On the one hand, it is one of the few dramas that remains loyal to Crocus in leaving out Joseph's father and brothers. On the other hand, when it comes to characterizing Potiphar's wife, Alinde, it exchanges Plautus and Terence for Euripides and Seneca. The result is a light-footed comedy filled with riddles and comic scenes, with at its heart a tragic female character whose passion, shame, and doubt almost drive her to suicide.

In both these dramas, a contrast becomes apparent between her and the rest of the story. In Gart's drama, the act in which she appears is demarcated from the rest of the play by its lack of exegetical commentary. In Montreux's comedy, there is a marked contrast between the tragic lamentations of the character and the humoristic scenes taking place around her.

A Tragic Character in the Spotlight

Pandolfo Collenuccio in Italian, Miguel de Carvajal in Spanish, Thiebold Gart in German, and Mikołaj Rey in Polish insert a tragic element into the episode with Potiphar's wife, but still tell Joseph's story in full. This is different in the Latin tragedy by the Polish playwright Simon Simonides. *Castus Joseph*, published in 1587, is a Senecan tragedy that is not only thoroughly classicizing in its lofty rhetorical style but also follows the structure of Euripides's *Hippolytos* closely.[76] Thus, Simonides is the first author who turns the confrontation between Joseph and Potiphar's wife into a classical tragedy. In contrast to Crocus, Macropedius, and Rochotius, his play does not end at the high point, with Joseph being released from prison, but at the low point, with Joseph being led to prison. In contrast to every other Joseph play, Joseph does not even appear that much in the play. He only appears in the first act, whereas most of the play is a dialogue between Iempsar (Potiphar's wife), her nurse, and the chorus. This is the first time that the whole play revolves around the character of Potiphar's wife, as a result of the parallel with Greek and Roman tragedy.

Two later authors also follow the model of *Phaedra*, but they both incorporate their tragedy within a Joseph trilogy containing the whole story. The first is the Lutheran pastor Theodorus Rhodius, whose collected Latin plays were published in 1625.[77] This short tragedy is a more traditional Joseph play than the one by Simonides in that it makes more room for Joseph himself. The second is the Dutch playwright Joost van den Vondel, who first translated Seneca's *Phaedra* in 1628 and then published his tragedy *Joseph in Egypten*, in the style of Seneca and Euripides, twelve years later.[78] The first part of Vondel's Joseph trilogy is his translation of Hugo Grotius's *Sophompaneas* (1635). Vondel also stays close to the scenic structure and sentiments of his Greek and Roman models, although his Joseph is a decidedly Christian hero.[79] In these three tragedies, however, the focus is on Potiphar's wife and her doomed struggle against her feelings.

The Evil Witch

Jean Lebeau describes how in 1572 German Joseph drama takes a new direction. In that year, the Alsatian schoolmaster Christian Zyrl publishes an extremely elaborate Joseph play in two parts that incorporates a lot of non-biblical material. This trend was already announced by

Macropedius's elaborate play. In the footsteps of Zyrl's success, and in line with a general trend in European drama, innovations in Joseph plays now consist of thematic digressions and comic additions rather than structural or stylistic innovations. In 1593 in Tübingen, Joseph Schlayss plagiarizes Zyrl's play and adds translated scenes from the Latin play by Hunnius (1584).[80] Aegidius Hunnius, professor of theology at Marburg, had written two plays in which he fleshes out the complete biblical story, with for instance no fewer than two scenes where Joseph receives the news that his wife has given birth.[81] The intrigue with Potiphar's wife, however, is a miniature version of Crocus's play in only one act.

Five authors who were then all living and working in Saxony and Silesia joined the new trend with their own German dramas in the decades around the turn of the century: the Meistersinger Adam Puschmann (1592); the school rectors Andreas Gasmann (1610), Martin Böhme (1609), and Josephus Goezius (1612); and the Catholic priest Balthasarus Voidius (1619). One source is especially prominent in providing new material for these plays. This is the apocryphal *Testament of the Twelve Patriarchs*, which purports to assemble the last words of each of Jacob's twelve sons.[82] Robert Grosseteste made a Latin translation from the Greek in the thirteenth century. His translation was printed in Augsburg in 1520. German translations were first printed in Strassburg in 1539 and 1596, in Augsburg in 1544, and in Frankfurt in 1569. The testament of Joseph, in particular, retells the episode with Potiphar's wife in detail and adds many new elements. In this version, and in the dramas inspired by it, Potiphar's wife is a malignant character who threatens to kill first Joseph and then her husband, does not shy away from promising to convert in exchange for sex, and tries to feed Joseph a magic potion to make him fall in love with her. Psychological depth is replaced with the stereotype of the evil witch.

Romantic Rivals

Like the German dramas, Spanish Joseph drama wanders off in a different direction from the biblical narrative, but it does so in its own specific way. It introduces many elements from medieval Jewish, Islamic, and Christian folklore. Although Carvajal's tragedy is a recurring presence in later Joseph plays, these plays, written for professional actors and pure entertainment rather than for didactic school performances, turn to romance rather than to tragedy.

In Spain, the character of Aseneth, the "daughter of the priest of On" whom Joseph marries after he becomes de facto ruler of Egypt, gains prominence over the character of Potiphar's wife. This is for instance the case in the *Auto de los desposorios de Joseph* (*Auto about the Marriage of Joseph*), from the third quarter of the sixteenth century.[83] In a play by Antonio Mira de Amescua from the second quarter of the seventeenth century, the first act cuts directly from the scene where Jacob mourns Joseph to the scene where Joseph explains Pharaoh's dreams and is promoted, thus leaving out the whole episode at Potiphar's house.[84] Calderon, in 1670, begins his play with Joseph in prison.[85] Both authors focus on the romance and marriage between Joseph and his future wife.

When Potiphar's wife does appear, she enters into a direct rivalry with Aseneth (who is sometimes her daughter), a fact that is used to comic effect. In the *Adversa y prospera fortuna de Joseph* (*The Misfortune and Prosperity of Joseph*) by Luis Velez de Guevara, dating to the first quarter of the seventeenth century, when Potiphar introduces Joseph in his house, not only his wife but also his daughter and their servant immediately fall in love with the newcomer.[86] All three women vie for his attention and get in each other's way. In one scene, Joseph receives three declarations of love by three different women. The anonymous *Los Triunfos de Joseph* from 1672 includes an intrigue with a love letter that falls into the wrong hands.[87] Last, there is the play by the Sephardic Amsterdam Jew Isaac de Matatia Aboab (1586/1587), which takes the story with the amorous rivalry between three women from Guevara, but adds a scene where Joseph saves Aseneth and her servant from a crocodile as well as an intrigue with a ring and veiled love declarations.[88] In all of these dramas, Zenobia is not an especially malignant but, rather, a scheming character who goes to great lengths to trump her love rival.

Love rivals and intrigue are also the defining element of Christian Weise's school play *Der Keusche Joseph* (1690). Similar to *Los Triunfos de Joseph*, the story is that of the romance between Joseph and Aseneth, leaving out completely Joseph's family story. *Der Keusche Joseph* contains the three women falling in love with Joseph, Arabian princes as love rivals, an intrigue with a letter, and many narrative additions about Egyptian court life.

Absence

The first extant Jesuit Joseph play is the one found in two versions from Dillingen (1579) and München (1582/1583).[89] The core of these plays is a plagiarized version of Macropedius with some changes and a bit of

Crocus mixed in, supplemented with the larger story of Joseph's brothers. These plays originate when Jesuit drama is still finding its identity. When in 1599, the Ratio Studiorum standardizes practices of Jesuit education, one of its regulations is the prohibition on female roles in school theater. As a result, the character of Potiphar's wife appears in none of the later Jesuit plays. The majority of the plays of which we have texts or titles even seem to leave out that part of the story completely. Many titles indicate that they treat either the episode where Joseph is sold by his brothers or the episode where he rules Egypt and forgives his brothers. In cases where Potiphar and his household do appear, scenic tricks keep the character of Potiphar's wife out of view. In Bidermann's play, for instance, the character is heard calling out to her servants from inside the house. The role comprises five words in total: "Famuli, servate; famuli" and "Suppetias famuli."[90] Crucius, Bidermann, and a few others show Joseph fleeing from the room where the assault happened: the same scene that Collenuccio, Carvajal, and Crocus introduced but without any of the confrontations leading to that moment.

Conclusion

Looking at Joseph plays from a European perspective, what changes for the character of Potiphar's wife in comparison to the account given by Lebeau and Wimmer? How do the plays from other regions and other languages relate to the strong central cluster of Dutch and German humanists writing in Latin and German? First of all, my overview confirms the wide-reaching transnational impact of the biblical plays by Dutch humanists such as Cornelius Crocus. When Mikołaj Rej, the first author to write exclusively in Polish, publishes his Joseph play, it leans heavily on Crocus and Macropedius. A century later, Lope de Vega, although making use of Carvajal, writes a Joseph play that is atypical for the Spanish cluster and that uses elements from the Dutch humanists. Even in the middle decades of the seventeenth century, two obscure Dutch plays, one from the north and one from the south, still use the comic model of Crocus. Authors of different confessional creeds take up the character of Sephirach, although there are certain demarcations between later reactions to the character. For instance, there is a marked tendency in Lutheran authors to reduce the character, or to vilify her and use her to teach a misogynist moral lesson. Eventually, this leads to the transformation of the character into an evil sorceress at the end of the sixteenth century.

Outside of this group, there is only one other cluster in which a different model of the character is developed collectively. This is the Spanish cluster, with the strong influence of romance. Despite Carvajal's continuing presence in later Spanish Joseph plays, his character Zenobia is supplanted by her rival and Joseph's future wife Aseneth. The only exceptions are Lope's play and the Mexican *auto historial* by Sor Juana Inez de la Cruz.

Spanish drama is characterized by the same predilection for extravagance and profuse narrative that we find in the German dramas that make such abundant use of the *Testament of the Twelve Patriarchs*, even if this predilection works with different narrative sources and produces very different characterizations of Potiphar's wife. Jesuit Joseph plays also take part in these dramatic trends, but without the character of Potiphar's wife. At the time when her character becomes ever more stereotyped in German school drama and Spanish romantic comedy, the Jesuits remove her completely from the stage.

The tragic model of Phaedra, introduced by Collenuccio and Carvajal, reoccurs repeatedly, breaking through Crocus's comic hegemony. Authors see a link between the mythical tragic character and the biblical woman. This characterization does not occur within a cluster: neither Collenuccio's nor Carvajal's tragic characters were received in the way that Crocus's Sephirach was. Rather, the tragic characterization is taken up now and then by individual authors and in different languages. In fact, the seven plays I have discussed in which Potiphar's wife is a tragic character are written in six different languages: Italian (Collenuccio), Spanish (Carvajal), German (Gart), Latin (by the Polish Simonides and the German Rhodius), and Dutch (Vondel). Last, the Swedish and English plays show that it is possible even in the seventeenth century to write a Joseph play that remains isolated from the innovations and complexities that the humanists introduced and of which the character of Potiphar's wife is a prime example.

Notes

1. This article was written within the scope of the NWO-funded project: "TransLatin: The Transnational Impact of Latin Theatre from the Early Modern Netherlands, a Qualitative and Computational Analysis" (https://translatin .nl). I want to thank the anonymous reviewer for their insightful comments.
2. Frederic Everett Faverty, "The Story of Joseph and Potiphar's Wife in Mediaeval Literature," *Studies and Notes in Philology and Literature* 13 (1931); Shalom Goldman, *The Wiles of Women/The Wiles of Men: Joseph and Potiphar's Wife in Ancient Near Eastern, Jewish, and Islamic Folklore* (Ann Arbor, MI: Albany State University of New York Press, 2016); Mieke Bal, *Loving Yusuf: Conceptual Travels from Present to Past* (Chicago: University of Chicago Press, 2008); Manfred Tiemann, *Josef und die Frau Potifars im populärkulturellen Kontext : transkulturelle*

Verflechtungen in Theologie, bildender Kunst, Literatur, Musik und Film (Wiesbaden: Springer, 2020).

3. Monia Mezzetti, *I volti della moglie di Putifarre nella letteratura francese (secc. XII–XX)* (Pisa: Edizioni ETS, 2010); John D. Yohannan, *Joseph and Potiphar's Wife in World Literature: An Anthology of the Story of the Chaste Youth and the Lustful Stepmother* (New York: New Directions, 1968).

4. Raymond Lebegue, *La tragédie religieuse en France: les débuts (1514–1573)* (Paris: Champion, 1929), 471.

5. Jean Lebeau, *Salvator mundi: l' "exemple" de Joseph dans le théâtre allemand au XVIe siècle* (Nieuwkoop: B. de Graaf, 1977); Ruprecht Wimmer, *Jesuitentheater: Didaktik und Fest: das Exemplum des ägyptischen Joseph auf den deutschen Bühnen der Gesellschaft Jesu* (Frankfurt am Main: Klostermann, 1982).

6. Lebeau, *Salvator mundi*, 285–349.

7. My corpus consists of circa 118 extant Joseph plays written between 1450 and 1700; I have no access to the texts or summaries of thirteen of these; Potiphar's wife appears in 55 of the other 105 plays.

8. Eduardo Melfi, "Collenuccio, Pandolfo," in *Dizionario Biografico degli Italiani*, 1982.

9. Elisa Curti, "'Per vostra utilitade e per diletto': la Comedia di Iacob e Ioseph di Pandolfo Collenuccio fra teatro di corte e sacra rappresentazione," in *Boiardo, il teatro, i cavalieri in scena: Atti del convegno Scandiano 15–16 maggio 2009*, ed. Giuseppe Anceschi and William Spaggiari (Novara: Interlinea edizioni, 2010), 130.

10. Victoria Moul, *A Guide to Neo-Latin Literature* (Cambridge: Cambridge University Press, 2017), 225.

11. Elisa Curti, "'Per vostra utilitade e per diletto,'" 131.

12. Pandolfo Collenuccio, *Comedia de Iacob: & de Iosep: composta dal magnifico caualiero e dottore: messere Pandolpho Collenutio da Pesaro ad instantia de lo illustris. & eccellentissimo. sig. ducha Hercole de Ferara in terza rima istoriata*, 1525.

13. Paolo Ventrone, "The Fifteenth-Century Florentine 'Sacra Rappresentazione,'" *European Medieval Drama* 24 (2020): 55–64.

14. Curti, "'Per vostra utilitade e per diletto,'" 133–35.

15. Curti, 142.

16. Curti, 144. "Collenuccio's text, charged with its sententious exemplarity, represents a significant experiment in sacred drama of the humanists, not comparable either to the sacred Florentine rappresentazioni, although they are known to him and from which he draws the Old Testament theme, nor to the tradition of religious staging of the north. The comedy seems to be looking for new expressions for religious theater, more classical and 'regular' [. . .]"

17. Ventrone, "The Fifteenth-Century Florentine 'Sacra Rappresentazione,'" 56.

18. "It is not a good time to be standing here, but hear my wish, / Isep; love me as I love you. / I leave you now, and I go with a wounded heart."

19. This reporting of actions by servants is used frequently throughout the play.

20. Pandolfo Collenuccio, *Operette Morali: Poesie Latine e Volgari*, ed. Alfredo Saviotti (Bari: G. Laterza & Figli, 1929), 194. "That if her love turns to hate there will be no snake more venomous than she. [. . .] She will continue to persecute him, like a famished tiger who cannot find food for her small cubs nor for herself."

21. Collenuccio, 194. "I was sitting in my room by myself / to go over my accounts and documents. / And there she assaults me, almost as in flight, / this impudent beast, and she puts / her hands on me without any respect, / to break my faithful chastity."

22. Lucius Annaeus Seneca, *Moral essays*, vol. 1, 3 vols. (Cambridge, MA: Harvard University Press, 2007).
23. Vincent Dupuis, "La furieuse, ou le spectacle de la fureur féminine dans la tragédie de la Renaissance," *Revue Ad Hoc* 1 (2012).
24. Dupuis.
25. Melveena MacKendrick, *Theatre in Spain 1490–1700* (Cambridge: Cambridge University Press, 1989), 40.
26. Michael D. McGaha, *The Story of Joseph in Spanish Golden Age Drama* (Lewisburg, PA, London: Bucknell University Press, Associated University Presses, 1998), 17.
27. McGaha, xxiv.
28. David M. Gitlitz, "Conversos and the Fusion of Worlds in Micael de Carvajal's Tragedia Josephina," *Hispanic Review* 40, no. 3 (1972): 260–70; Charles Patterson, "A New Look at the Converso Problem in Carvajal's Tragedia Josephina," *EHumanista: Journal of Iberian Studies*, no. 17 (2011): 349–65; McGaha, *The Story of Joseph in Spanish Golden Age Drama*, 1998.
29. Micael de Carvajal, *Tragedia Josephina*, ed. Joseph E. Gillet (Princeton: Princeton University Press, 1932), lvi.
30. "How can this be, / me being such a lady, / and my husband adoring me / with vehement love, / that I let myself be overcome by a boy, and a foreigner, / my slave and my prisoner! / I cannot believe it." Carvajal, *Tragedia Josephina*, 78.
31. Carvajal, 79. "Oh I don't know what to do! / Should I speak to him or leave him alone, / should I aggress him or weary him out, / to find a remedy for my affliction?"
32. Carvajal, 80–81.
33. Carvajal, xli–xliii.
34. James Rothschild, *Le mistère du Viel Testament* (Paris: Firmin Didot, 1878), 51–67.
35. Rothschild, 67.
36. Carvajal, *Tragedia Josephina*, 86.
37. Carvajal, 90. "Do not look down that way / on me, your mistress. / Treat me as a Moorish girl. / Come here, you idiot. / Consider me as your equal / and even as your servant."
38. Carvajal, 92.
39. Carvajal, 93. "Embrace me and I will not go through with it. / You don't want to? Then you die."
40. Carvajal, lvi.
41. Carvajal, lvi.
42. Albertus Josefus Kölker, "Alardus Aemstelredamus en Cornelius Crocus, twee Amsterdamse priester-humanisten; hun leven, werken en theologische opvattingen. Bijdrage tot de kennis van het humanisme in Noord-Nederland in de eerste helft van de zestiende eeuw" (Nijmegen: Dekker & Van de Vegt, 1963); Jan Bloemendal, *Cornelius Crocus. Ioseph: editie met inleiding, vertaling en aantekeningen, Scaenica Amstelodamensia* (Florivallis, 2010).
43. Lebeau, *Salvator mundi*, 310–11.
44. Jan Bloemendal, *Cornelius Crocus. Ioseph: editie met inleiding, vertaling en aantekeningen, Scaenica Amstelodamensia* (Florivallis, 2010), 94. "Do I look good enough like this? Does this dress suit me? I did put a lot of work into it. I spent the whole day doing my make-up and dressing myself."
45. Bloemendal, *Cornelius Crocus. Ioseph*, 94. "My Joseph, my beloved, my life, my only desire."

46. "There she goes again."
47. James A. Parente, *Religious Drama and the Humanist Tradition: Christian Theater in Germany and in the Netherlands, 1500–1680* (Leiden and New York: Brill, 1987), 31.
48. Bloemendal, *Cornelius Crocus. Ioseph*, 112. "Shall I suffer a slave to mock me without punishment? / I would rather be dead."
49. "Just wait, you jerk."
50. The typological parallel with Christ remaining silent before Pilate might also play a role.
51. Bloemendal, *Cornelius Crocus. Ioseph*, 142. "Because it is unworthy for me to speak, master."
52. Collenuccio, *Operette Morali*, 370–72.
53. Carvajal, *Tragedia Josephina*, xix–xxvii.
54. Carvajal, xxix–xxxii.
55. The first is the *Comoediae ac tragoediae aliquot ex Novo et Vetere Testamento Desumptae* by Nicholas Brylinger and the second the *Dramata sacra: Comoediae atque tragoediae aliquot è Veteri Testamento desumptae* by Johannes Oporinus.
56. Parente, *Religious Drama and the Humanist Tradition*.
57. Wimmer, *Jesuitentheater*, 98–99.
58. Lebeau, *Salvator mundi*, 326.
59. Angela Škovierová, "Slovak Humanist Ondrej Rochotský (ca. 1583–1623) and His Works Stored in the Wrocław University Library," *Z Badań Nad Książką i Księgozbiorami Historycznymi* 12 (2018): 69–88; Andreas Rochotius, *Josephiados comœdia ex Genesis lib: cap: 39.40.41* (Prague: Typis Schumanianis, 1608).
60. Lebeau, *Salvator mundi*, 735–36.
61. Xystus Betuleius, *Susanna Comoedia Tragica* (Köln: Johann I. Gymnich, 1538), 9–10.
62. Jacob Ruf, *Ein hüpsch nü=‖wes Spil von Josephen ‖ dem fromen Jüngling/ vß etlichen ‖ Capitlen deß büchs der Gschöpfften ‖ gezogen/ insonders lustig vnd ‖ nutzlich zeläsen.‖* (Zürich: Augustin Fries, 1549), 76.
63. Gerda Hagenau, *Polnisches Theater und Drama: ein integraler Bestandteil europäischer Theaterkultur 966–1795* (Wien: Böhlau, 2000), 228–29.
64. Lope de Vega, *Obras de Lope de Vega. VI–VIII: Autos y coloquios.*, vol. VIII, Biblioteca de autores españoles desde la formación del lenguaje hasta nuestros días 157 (Madrid: Atlas, 1963).
65. Maarten F. van Dijck, "Botsende belangen: de zielzorg in enkele norbertijnenparochies in het Hageland gedurende de zeventiende en achttiende eeuw," *Analecta Praemonstratensia* 82, no. 1/4 (2006): 321–46; Willem Zeebots, *Neder-duytsche gedichten* (Leuven: By de weduwe van B. Maes, 1662).
66. "There is no worse pest than an evil woman. / No devil in hell can do more harm, / and most of the harm that he does, he does through women."
67. Johannes von Travers, *Joseph: Engadinisches Drama des XVI. Jahrhunderts* (Zürich: Zürcher & Furrer, 1891).
68. Joachim Greff, *Ein Lieblich Vnd Nuetzbarlich Spiel von Dem Patriarchen Jacob Vnd Seinen Zwelff Sönen* (Magdeburg: [Lotter], 1535).
69. Lebeau, *Salvator mundi*, 336.
70. Thomas Petri Gevaliensis, *Josephi historia: ånyo af trycket utgifven* (Stockholm: V. Levertin, 1849).
71. Carleton Fairchild Brown, *The Stonyhurst Pageants* (Göttingen: Vandenhoeck & Ruprecht, 1920); J. Case Tompkins, "Old Testament Adaptation in 'The Stonyhurst Pageants,'" *Early Theatre* 16, no. 1 (2013): 119–37; Hardin Craig, "Terentius Christianus and the Stonyhurst Pageants," *Philological Quarterly*

2 (1923): 56. The Stonyhurst Pageants generally follow the Bible closely, except for the Naaman play, which is a translation of the play by the Dutch humanist Cornelius Schonaeus.

72. Juana Inés de la Juana Inés de la Cruz, *Auto historial alegórico "El cetro de José,"* ed. Alfonso Méndez Plancarte (México: Fondo de Cultura Económica, 1955).
73. Thiebold Gart, *Joseph: Ein Schöne Und Fruchtbare Comedia* (Straßburg, 1540); Connie Theresa Collier Allison, "Thiebolt Gart's 'Joseph': An Analysis of a German Sixteenth-Century Drama" (Austin: University of Texas, 1972).
74. Lebeau, *Salvator mundi*, 332.
75. Nicolas de Montreux, *Joseph le Chaste, Comédie* (Hachette Livre BNF, 2016); Daniela Mauri, "Joseph le chaste de Nicolas de Montreux Une 'comédie sainte' multiforme" (Paris: Classiques Garnier, 2018), 313–25.
76. Jan Bloemendal, *Rhetoric and Early Modern Latin Drama. The Two Tragedies by the "Polish Pindar" Simon Simonides (1558–1629): Castus Ioseph and Pentesilea, Rhetoric and Drama* (Berlin, Munich, Boston: De Gruyter, 2017), 120; Simon Simonides, *Castus Ioseph* (Kraków: Drukarnia Łazarzowa, 1587).
77. Theodorus Rhodius, *Theodori Rhodii Germani Dramata sacra* (Straßburg: P. Ledertz, 1625).
78. Joost van den Vondel, *Joseph in Egypten: Treurspel.* (Amsterdam: Dominicus vander Stichel, 1640).
79. W. A. P. Smit, *Van Pascha tot Noah: een verkenning van Vondels drama's naar continuiteit en ontwikkeling in hun grondmotief en structuur* (Zwolle: Tjeenk Willink, 1956), 1:355–85.
80. Christian Zyrl and Joseph Schlayss, *Joseph: Die Gantze Historia von Dem from[m]En Und Keuschen Joseph, Wie Er von Seinen Brüdern Verkaufft, Vnnd Die Kinder Jsrael in Egypten Kommen Sind. Nach Biblischem Text . . . in Ein Schöne, Christliche Vnnd Nutzliche Comoediam Erstlich Gestelt* (Tübingen: Georg Gruppenbach, 1593).
81. Aegidius Hunnius, *Iosephus: comoedia sacra* (Strasbourg: Bertram, 1597).
82. Marinus de Jonge, *Testamenta XII patriarcharum* (Leiden: Brill, 1970).
83. Nicolás González Ruiz, *Piezas maestras del teatro teológico español,* 4th ed., vol. 1 (Madrid: Biblioteca de Autores Cristianos, 1997).
84. Antonio Mira de Amescua and Agustín de la Granja, "El más feliz cautiverio y los sueños de Josef," in *Teatro completo* (Granada: Universidad de Granada-Diputación de Granada, 2010), 10:361–454.
85. Pedro Calderón de la Barca, *Sueños hay que verdad son,* ed. Michael D. McGaha, Teatro del Siglo de Oro 86 (Pamplona, Kassel: Universidad de Navarra, Edition Reichenberger, 1997).
86. Luis Vélez de Guevara, "La Próspera y Adversa Fortuna de Joseph: Comedia Famosa," MSS/15151, Biblioteca Nacional de España, Madrid.
87. "Los Triunfos de Joseph: Comedia Famosa" (n.d.), T/20092, Biblioteca Nacional de España, Madrid.
88. Aboab, Isaac de Matatia, "Comedia / de La Vida y Sucessos / de Josseph / Llamado El Perseguido Dichozo / Relacion Muy Agradavel / En Que Se Refieren / Todas Las Tragedias y Grandezas / Que Por Dicho" (Amsterdam, 1686), EH 48 D 21, Ets Haim, Amsterdam; McGaha, *The Story of Joseph in Spanish Golden Age Drama,* 226–32.
89. Wimmer, *Jesuitentheater,* 117–57.
90. "Servants, come save me, servants!" and "Help, servants!"

Royal Netherlands Academy of Arts and Sciences, Huygens ING
dinah.wouters@huygens.knaw.nl

Review Notices

Illuminating Jesus in the Middle Ages. Edited by Jane Beal (Commentaria: Sacred Texts and Their Commentaries, 12). Leiden: Brill, 2019. Pp. 374.

Because the figure of Jesus is so pervasive throughout medieval culture, medievalists have at times tended to take as a given the influence of this illustrious figure on the medieval authors, artists, political figures, and other actors they study. Scholars have also tended to shy away from comprehensive treatments of medieval devotion to and views of Jesus and, in fact, seem to have focused more recently on the Virgin Mary. There are authors of monographs that touch upon or delve more deeply into issues and themes related to Christ. However, in general, these books do not carefully track, in their indexes, their references to the medieval cult of Jesus. Some do not include an entry with the heading "Jesus" at all. The present reviewer perceived this rather frustrating tendency when studying medieval representations of and responses to Jesus's childhood and medieval Christology more broadly. She is thus pleased that Jane Beal has likewise noticed and responded to the curious lack of published scholarship that explicitly explores and concertedly treats the reception of Jesus at different times and in different places over the course of the medieval period. More specifically, Beal has begun remedying the situation with her recent essay collection *Illuminating Jesus in the Middle Ages.* Building upon the monumental work of Caroline Walker Bynum (beginning in the 1980s and continuing to the present) and the many medievalists who have followed in her wake, as well as taking inspiration, more generally, from Jaroslav Pelikan's historical overview of the ways in which different cultures in different ages responded to the figure and person of Jesus (*Jesus through the Centuries: His Place in the History of Culture* [New Haven: Yale University Press, 1985]), Beal has collected a very useful group of sixteen essays of the highest scholarly caliber dealing with medieval approaches and responses to Jesus primarily in western Europe at different moments and in different medieval works. Her collection emphasizes exegetical, hagiographical, visionary, and literary

Medievalia et Humanistica, New Series, Number 47 (Reinhold F. Glei and Maik Goth, eds.), Rowman & Littlefield, 2022.

texts (with unfortunately little attention paid to artistic works, including manuscript illuminations of Jesus, and none to late-medieval drama).

Setting the stage for what follows, Beal's introduction provides a good basic, though very concise, overview of Christian culture in the Middle Ages, prior to summarizing each of the chapters within the volume. Indeed, she offers a primer of medieval Christianity somewhat reminiscent of Dee Dyas's book *Images of Faith in English Literature, 700–1500: An Introduction* (London: Longman, 1997). This introduction would be particularly useful for general readers and also students (both undergraduate and graduate) who might not already be familiar with how Christocentric medieval culture was, especially in terms of its social structure, its understanding and ritualization of time, and its approach to the Scriptures. Beal does well to emphasize that details concerning the life of Jesus were transmitted and the duty of honoring him was inculcated not only through the reading of the New Testament in monastic, scholastic, and Latin liturgical (musical) settings—a privilege of the few—but also by many other forms of media as well as the very conventions of medieval culture (such as the cruciform shape of churches, p. 5). Given that many essays in this user-friendly collection deal with interpretations of the Bible and the appropriation of biblical texts for meditation, prayer, and the liturgy, one who reads even just a few of the essays will learn much about how medieval Christians employed the Bible to nourish, express, and explore their faith. Readers will also learn that they found the Scriptures a rich source of ideas and images that inspired the development of their intellectual and creative talents, and also helped them understand and cope with their current situations. The same holds true, to a lesser extent, for biblically related legends.

Although some of the essays touch upon apocryphal and imaginative elaborations of scenes and personages from the Bible, the collection, in my view, could have dealt more specifically with the crucial roles played by the widely influential apocryphal texts known as the *Gospel of Nicodemus* and the *Gospel of Pseudo-Matthew* (neither of which appears in the index, but see the work of Zbigniew Izydorczyk, Brandon W. Hawk, and Mary Dzon, among others, for more details). This is to say that greater stress could have been placed on the legendary, not simply biblical, Jesus. Furthermore, while the volume does, indeed, provide a capacious view of different approaches to and views of Jesus, readers searching for Jewish and Islamic responses to Jesus and his followers will not find them here (though the collection does give some attention to the unfortunate anti-Judaic corollary of medieval Christ-centered devotion, especially that focused on Jesus's Passion). In addition, blatantly unorthodox Christian responses to Jesus and aspects of his cult are not the central concern of any one essay or treated in a sustained way, though Michael P. Kuczynski and Paul J. Patterson discuss Wycliffite challenges to the views and practices of the Catholic majority in late-medieval England, while Donna Trembinski briefly mentions the Waldensians and Linda Stone the thirteenth-century Dominicans' concern with heresy. Rob Lutton, however, does give substantial attention to the late-medieval unease about the "perceived idolatry" (p. 147) of devotion to the Holy Name, especially the sacred monogram. By pointing out the general absence of alternative perspectives on Jesus, however, I do not wish to imply that the collection is deficient, but rather to suggest ways in which "the Christological ideal" of the Middle Ages (a phrase used by Beal, pp. 3–4) could be further nuanced in subsequent studies.

Another minor quibble the present reviewer has with the volume is that a small handful of the essays do not seem aimed at a general audience but presuppose an audience already fairly well-versed in the specific field or text(s) with which their essay deals. So even though, throughout the volume, a helpful bibliography is provided in the footnotes, and all of the quotations from the primary sources are offered with translations (which usually appear below passages cited in the original languages), with the significance of such quotes typically well explained, in the case of a few of the essays, one suspects that many readers would profit from them more fully only after a rereading, perhaps returning to them after carefully reading at least select passages from the primary sources under consideration, within their contexts, and after sampling some of the relevant scholarship. As a result of the fact that a few of the contributors apparently approached their task more as specialists than as teachers instructing and enlightening curious readers who come to the collection with different degrees of knowledge, the volume seems to have a somewhat uneven texture. Nevertheless, the book offers much illumination for those who wisely choose what to read based upon their familiarity with the sources and their own current interests and needs.

This is not a dull, monolithic volume. Here we find a healthy balance of pieces that, on the one hand, focus on a given author or closely related texts (for example, Bede, the Irish poet Blathmac, Dante, Julian of Norwich, and Middle English commentaries on the Psalms) and those that, on the other, offer a broader survey of Christological themes or issues. These include essays that explore the myth of the virgin's capture of the unicorn that signifies the Incarnation (Beal), the soul's yearning for Christ the Bridegroom (Galloway), and the indebtedness of the Feast of Corpus Christi to Juliana of Mont Cornillon's affective devotion to the humanity and Eucharistic presence of Christ (Zimbalist).

The present reviewer, for her part, particularly enjoyed and learned much from the essays by Lutton and Trembinksi, to single out just a couple. Lutton's survey of the emergence and development of devotion to the Holy Name in the medieval West, the second-longest essay in the collection, traces approaches to the name of Jesus of well-known figures such as Bernard of Clairvaux, Richard Rolle, Henry Suso, and Bernardino of Siena, among others, as well the emergence of the sacred monogram IHS (and its other forms) as a cultic "imagetext" (p. 151). The overview given in this chapter definitely provides a much needed up-to-date, and wonderfully thorough, treatment of the topic in English. Whereas Rob Lutton successfully covers much ground, Donna Trembinski insightfully explores a smaller range of sources, offering a close reading of select texts by Francis of Assisi as well as early hagiographical texts about Francis and his followers. These early Franciscan sources can at times seem repetitive and quite similar to a non-expert, but Trembinski masterfully elucidates their key differences through close reading, while keeping a finely tuned question at the forefront: in what sense did Francis reflect Christ? (And further, we might ask, how in drawing others to himself did Francis, a charismatic figure, lead them to his Master?) Given the scholarly commonplace of the growing emphasis on the humanity of Christ in the later Middle Ages (which the volume in several places refers to, using the term "affective piety"), one might assume that any seriously devout medieval Christian would have sought to engage in some form of *imitatio Christi.* Yet Trembinski helpfully distinguishes between Francis's apparent view of himself as following in the footsteps of Christ as his humble disciple and the attempt of Francis's more stringent followers to portray him as an *alter Christus,* whose very steps they felt they had to retrace dutifully and carefully. (It is worth noting that the complexity of the concept "imitatio Christi," which is sometimes flattened by scholars' frequent use of the term as a catchword, is highlighted by Trembinski's nuanced discussion here, which recalls Giles Constable's meticulous exposition of the topic in his book, *Three Studies in Medieval Religious and Social Thought* [Cambridge: Cambridge University Press, 1995], a work not cited in this volume but certainly complementary to it.) Furthermore, Trembinski's essay, as well as a few others in the collection that focus on the writings by or about holy people (such as Barbara Zimbalist's on Juliana of Mont Cornillon or Aaron Canty's on Gertrude the Great), lead us to consider the wider question of how medieval holy people (as refracted in the sources) could seemingly be such unique individuals with strong personalities and firm viewpoints, and yet serve as self-effacing, moonlike reflections of the Sun of Justice, one of the many medieval titles for Christ. (Peter Damian, e.g., calls Mary the "star . . . through whom the Sun of Justice illuminated the world," PL 144:753; cf. John 8:12, where Jesus asserts that he is the light of the world.)

To be sure, if a scholarly project were to try to cover numerous medieval holy persons who sought to mold their lives after the teachings and actions of Christ, as well as myriad aspects of medieval religiosity ultimately rooted in the love of and commitment to Christ, it would result in several books rather than something that could fit between two covers. In a similar way, medieval Christian scholars' belief that Jesus was to be found throughout the Scriptures (hence Jerome's famous remark that ignorance of them was ignorance of Christ, PL 24:17) resulted in not just a single allegorical reading of the whole Bible (useful though the *Glossa ordinaria* was as a repository of key interpretations of biblical texts), but in countless writings and creative works of many kinds, as well as performative practices, all of which, in some way, sought to elucidate and celebrate the mysterious and incarnate Word of God. Beal thus rightfully acknowledges that the various contributions to the volume ("like matches set to a candle wick," p. 24) taken together in no way offer a comprehensive treatment but rather are meant to inspire future scholarship on the development of various views of Christ over the course of the medieval centuries.

While Beal, for the most part, graciously leaves the task of making grand generalizations to her readers, the essays she has gathered and sequenced chronologically do suggest that, early on, the figure of Jesus was generally more adapted to fit the expectations, ideals, and needs of males concerned with strength and power and the maintenance of the social order during precarious times. Moreover, early on, when the process of the conversion of Northern peoples was still ongoing, the figure of Christ was sometimes appropriated syncretistically so as to make him seem more familiar to those enmeshed in pagan culture (pp. 70–71). In contrast, in the high and later Middle Ages, with the increasing emphasis on the humanity of Christ and the flourishing of female spirituality, Christians tended to concentrate their efforts and desires more on imitating and achieving an intimate union with the human (and, for many medieval women, markedly male) Christ. Jesus was then seen more as someone who had come down to their level, out of tender compassion and love, than as a mighty lord who could rescue them from their weakness and misery by battling and overcoming the forces of evil. Hence we might well posit an emotional shift on the part of Jesus's admirers and devotees over the course of the Middle Ages from reverential awe to tender sympathy and intense yearning, a development previously noted by other scholars.

Last, the volume very helpfully includes a detailed index plus a full bibliography that separates primary and secondary sources and also provides a short list of manuscripts cited by the contributors. All of this material will undoubtedly serve as a springboard for further reflection and scholarship within this vast multidisciplinary field of study, yet greater care could have been taken to iron out some of the inconsistencies and remove some of the infelicities contained therein, including the misplacement of items (e.g., a number of secondary works appear in the section of primary works), occasional irregular methods of citation, mistakes with Latin and other foreign languages, misspellings of names, and typographical errors—all occurring frequently enough (in the bibliography and also to a lesser extent in the body of the volume) to become distracting. In addition, the manuscripts are not arranged according to city and archive, as they customarily are, but according to the original author (or title) of a text contained in the manuscript cited by one of the contributors. Despite these minor problems, this collection on the whole is an excellent work of scholarship that will be eminently useful for years to come, as scholars and students alike seek to gain a better understanding of the many ways medieval Christians sought to respond to the mysterious God-man who came to earth to dwell among their kind and was believed to have left a palpable presence of himself in the Church, and in culture, throughout the ages.

Mary Dzon
University of Tennessee
mdzon@utk.edu

Sari Kivistö, *Lucubrationes Neolatinae: Readings of Neo-Latin Dissertations and Satires* (Commentationes Humanarum Litterarum, 134). Helsinki: Societas Scientiarum Fennica, 2018. Pp. XII + 244.

In recent years, the study of early modern disputations has gained more and more scholarly attention. As disputations were held and defended at every university in the early modern age, the total number of disputations printed in Europe must be indeed staggering: Of these, ca. one hundred thousand have come down to us from the German cultural space, and another twenty-five thousand from Scandinavia.[1] These texts were generally written in Latin as exercises or to obtain an academic degree, and are hence sometimes derivative of or repeat typical textbook material. It is because of these characteristics that early modern disputations have long been labeled as "a tedious mass product"[2] and have been considered unworthy of serious academic study. As they are usually dispersed between libraries, it is laborious to gain a good overview of the extant material. Thanks to digital databases and the digitization efforts of many libraries, this material is now much more readily accessible, and new opportunities have arisen to reevaluate previous attitudes. In addition to standard textbook material, disputations also occasionally feature highly original discussions, as these texts were regularly used to test out new ideas or argue against old ones. In several ways disputations in the early modern period functioned in the academic world as journal articles do nowadays. Also, the vast number and derivative nature of the disputations have surprisingly proven to be an advantage in the study of intellectual history. Disputations were usually compulsory for all university students to attend and had to be approved by the deans of the faculties; thus these texts offer a quite accurate image of the everyday teaching environment at early modern universities. We can better understand what was taught to the educated elites of the period, and these texts line out the academic consensus far better than monograph-length treatments by allegedly exceptional authors. At the same time, disputations reflect the intellectual currents of the time, so studying the development of the themes in disputations permits us to follow the changes in academic tastes and the reception of new ideas.

In recent years, several books have focused on disputations;[3] additionally, there are various ongoing efforts to build (electronic) tools to study them better. Kivistö's book fits well into these recent endeavors, presenting some new material and gathering previously published articles that

Medievalia et Humanistica, New Series, Number 47 (Reinhold F. Glei and Maik Goth, eds.), Rowman & Littlefield, 2022.

in some way use disputations as source material. Focusing mainly on literary topics, the articles in Kivistö's book highlight the different directions disputations could take and show how we can use the material for case studies but also for more general observations. Of the twelve chapters of the book, nine have previously been published elsewhere and appear here in expanded or modified form.

The first chapter of the book deals with sympathy and discusses its use in two disputations that were presented at the academy of Turku toward the end of eighteenth century. These texts rely on the tradition of British moral philosophy and draw a connection between moral and aesthetical judgment. Kivistö here demonstrates how the knowledge about sentimentalist philosophical currents was presented in a Finnish academic setting. New ideas were often tested in disputations, and the material was used to teach students about philosophical currents.

The second chapter discusses two legal disputations from Germany that take jesting and practical jokes as their subject; the third chapter continues this theme, discussing people who laugh too much and people who do not laugh at all. Such humorous and curious topics or texts that approach their subject in tongue-in-cheek manner were often just a playful show of erudition and meant to amuse the fellow professors and students. We can find a whole catalog of such disputations in Sigmund Jacob Apin's *Unvorgreiffliche Gedancken*,[4] which lists disputations about dogs, beards, sausages, love letters, and so on. Such amusing subjects could, however, touch upon important issues as is evident from Christian Thomasius's legal disputation about ghosts, which has wider metaphysical and theological implications.

Continuing the mixture of serious curiosity and playfulness, chapter 4 treats the medical ideas of German physician Georg Franck von Franckenau. In the course of his career, he presided over several disputations that took strange themes as their focus, e.g., castration of women, eating glass, face punching, and the effects of purgatives. Similarly, his posthumous *Satyrae medicae* exhibits interest in oddities, but also presents an opportunity to demonstrate erudition and medical knowledge: it discusses ideas about prepuce, sexual difference, and menstruation and offers counterexamples to various theories about the physiology of men and women.

Chapters 4 and 5 discuss striving for innovation together with the concept of novelty and also utopianism. These chapters have theological and critical undertones, as novelty and utopianism relate to the current affairs and use the ideal state as a mirror, which often results in critique of the *status quo*. Chapters 7, 8 and 9 examine attitudes toward controversial books, plagiarism, forgeries, and forgers. These discussions are also highly interesting and relevant today, and describe the development of historical method and theory in the early modern period.

In the tenth chapter, Kivistö discusses the genre of satirical apotheosis and how it was used to subvert authority in antiquity and in the early modern period. In this article, she illustrates the critical attitude toward theologians in Erasmus's *Julius Exclusus*. It could, however, also be argued that Erasmus is generally very careful in his wording and might side with theology's criticism of worldly matters.[5] The book ends with chapters about apotheosis and poetic immortality, and elaborates how classical satire was used in the early years of the independent Republic of Finland.

Kivistö's book works well as an insight into early modern academic thinking, with the stress on the strange and curious, as the book title suggests. Her understanding of satire is very much in line with her discussion of Georg Franck von Franckenau's medical satires, where satire is understood not as a critical or didactic piece, but more as a kind of miscellany or medley. In this sense, the contents of her book conform well to the genre and offer sometimes the same kind of bewilderment and amusement as her early modern counterparts. However, a certain unevenness and brevity is typical of this genre, so the reader is often left with the desire for more fleshed-out and elaborated expositions. One can only hope that Kivistö will soon write something more substantial on these topics.

Notes

1. Cf. Manfred Komorowski, "Bibliotheken," in *Quellen zur frühneuzeitlichen Universitätsgeschichte: Typen, Bestände, Forschungsperspektiven*, ed. Ulrich Rasche, Wolfenbütteler Forschungen 128 (Wiesbaden: Harrassowitz, 2011), 55–66; Bo Lindberg, "Om dissertationer," in *Bevara för framtiden. Texter från en seminarieserie om specialsamlingar*, ed. Peter Sjökvist (Uppsala: Uppsala University, 2016) 13–39.
2. Manfred Komorowski, "Die alten Hochschulschriften: lästige Massenware oder ungehobene Schätze unserer Bibliotheken?," *Informationsmittel für Bibliotheken* 5 (1997): 379–400.
3. E.g., Axel Hörstedt, *Latin Dissertations and Disputations in the Early Modern Swedish Gymnasium. A Study of a Latin School Tradition c. 1620–c. 1820* (Göteborg: Göteborgs universitet, 2018); Marion Gindhart, Hanspeter Marti, and Robert Seidel, eds., *Frühneuzeitliche Disputationen* (Köln: Böhlau Köln, 2016); Robert Seidel, Hanspeter Marti, and Meelis Friedenthal, eds., *Early Modern Disputations and Dissertations in an Interdisciplinary and European Context*, Intersections: Interdisciplinary Studies in Early Modern Culture (Leiden: Brill, 2020).

4. Siegmund Jacob Apin, *Unvorgreiffliche Gedancken, wie man so wohl alte als neue Dissertationes academicas mit Nutzen sammlen, und einen guten Indicem darüber halten soll* (Nürnberg: Johann Daniel Tauber, 1719).
5. Desiderius Erasmus, *Collected Works of Erasmus. 5: Literary and Educational Writings Panegyricus, Moria, Julius Exclusus, Institutio Principis Christiani, Querela Pacis*, ed. A. H. T. Levi (Toronto: University of Toronto Press, 1986), 182–83.

Meelis Friedenthal
University of Tartu
meelis.friedenthal@ut.ee

Stephan Heilen, *Konjunktionsprognostik in der Frühen Neuzeit. Band 1: Die Antichrist-Prognose des Johannes von Lübeck (1474) zur Saturn-Jupiter-Konjunktion von 1504 und ihre frühneuzeitliche Rezeption* (Saecula Spiritalia, 53). Baden-Baden: Verlag Valentin Koerner, 2020. Pp. XII + 710.

This book is the first volume of a planned trilogy on astrological prognostics by conjunctions of planets. In early modern times, astrology was a widespread phenomenon, but astrologers were mostly concerned with individual horoscopes. A different subject, which is not yet treated sufficiently by scholars, is prediction of global events (natural disasters, pandemics, and especially the rise of a new religion) by means of planetary movements. Conjunctions occur when the inner planets, which move faster, pass the outer ones, and combine the astrological power of each other. The lack of studies in this field is due to its manifold implications, viz. mathematics, astronomy, history, theology and other disciplines, not to mention the necessary command of source languages (Latin, Greek, Arabic, Persian, and others). Not surprisingly, only a small number of persons today are able to treat that subject, fitting into the early modern profile of a *Universalgelehrter*. Fortunately, Stephan Heilen is such a person, and the scientific community can be happy that he undertook this task. Of course, it is not nearly possible to appreciate the whole project in the manner it deserves. What I can offer here is only a glimpse of the book's scope, content, and richness.

The first volume deals with the very first printed prediction of the Antichrist, written by a certain Johannes von Lübeck and published in Padua in 1474. It contains prolific astronomical calculations regarding the conjunctions of the outer planets, Saturn and Jupiter, which occur approximately every twenty years. According to the doctrine of the Persian-Arab mathematician and astronomer Abu Maʿshar (ninth century CE), whose works were translated into Latin in the twelfth century, there are important conjunctions only every 240 years, when Saturn and Jupiter enter a new "triplicity" of zodiac signs (a group of three signs associated with a corresponding element, i.e., fire, earth, air, and water). In Johannes's times, the next conjunction of that kind was calculated to happen on September 26, 1563. This date, however, was quite late, and therefore Johannes looked for an earlier *coniunctio maxima, que significat prophetam* ("a great conjunction that signifies the coming of a prophet"; see Heilen, p. 177). He found it by using a different astrological theory, put forward by Māshā'allāh ibn Atharī (late eighth century),

Medievalia et Humanistica, New Series, Number 47 (Reinhold F. Glei and Maik Goth, eds.), Rowman & Littlefield, 2022.

and declared the conjunction of June 10, 1504, to be the initial cause for the birth of the Antichrist. He will be born—as Johannes von Lübeck states—on September 14, 1506, to a Jewish woman and will appear (at the age of thirty) in 1536 as a false Messiah and a caricature of Jesus Christ. Three and a half years later, in March 1540, he will be defeated and killed by God.

In the introduction, Heilen presents his project and underlines the importance of editing, commenting, and discussing premodern texts on astrology, especially the doctrine of planetary conjunctions, which has been underestimated so far. Besides the conjunction of 1504 treated in the first volume, Heilen is going to deal with the conjunctions of 1484 (vol. 2) and of 1503/1504, where also Mars is involved (vol. 3). Most commendably, Heilen provides useful information on premodern knowledge of astronomical facts, methodology, and basic assumptions of astrology. The main part of the book is a detailed study of Johannes's *Prognosticum*, which can be truly called exhaustive. It informs not only about the work itself, but also about its scientific and historical context; about special astrological and demonological doctrines relevant to the Antichrist; and about the language and style of the treatise, its textual tradition in print and manuscript; and it provides a critical edition along with a German translation and a thorough commentary. Moreover, a long chapter on the reception of the *Prognosticum* in the late fifteenth century has been added. After it became clear that the prediction had failed, the *Prognosticum* was put on the index of prohibited books (first in 1557).

The merits of Heilen's book cannot be praised enough, and it is no exaggeration to call it a peak in interdisciplinary studies of early modern times. Admittedly, it is not easy for the non-expert reader to work through the book, but scholars of any discipline will have much benefit from it (or even parts of it) anyway. One of Heilen's most important findings, however, is—at least to my view—the detection of manipulation. Albeit with some caveats, it is convincingly demonstrated that Johannes von Lübeck "rectified" and even intentionally falsified astronomical data in order to support his prediction. More precisely: the author not only combined different theories and modes of calculation (as is common in early modern science), as well as "embellished" the observational data (as is perhaps excusable), but also obviously forged the horoscope of the Saturn-Jupiter conjunction by giving wrong positions to Mars and Venus, which were also important to make the conjunction a "great one." This shows that his motive was not primarily religious belief (or superstition), but rather "filthy Mammon." Johannes's main goal, as Heilen points out, was to gain a wealthy patron, namely, Kaiser Friedrich III. It seems that he dedicated a later version (now lost) to the emperor, as is attested by Johannes von Glogau (around 1500).

In sum: this book is a masterpiece, and it is only the first part of a trilogy. We hope that volumes 2 and 3 will see the light of day in the near future. In March 2020, Heilen predicted that they will be published "within a few years" (p. 34). Perhaps he can provide a more precise date by means of conjunction prognostics? The last conjunction of Saturn and Jupiter took place on December 21, 2020, in Aquarius, entering a new "triplicity."

Reinhold F. Glei
Ruhr-Universität Bochum
reinhold.glei@rub.de

Thomas Honegger, *Introducing the Medieval Dragon* (Medieval Animals). Cardiff: University of Wales Press, 2019. Pp. XVI. + 169. 1 color plate, 15 halftones.

Introducing the Medieval Dragon by Thomas Honegger is the inaugural monograph in Diane Heath and Victoria Blud's Medieval Animals series at the University of Wales Press. This addition to the ever-growing list of publications on this fantastic beast is a concise and levelheaded primer that contextualizes the dragon in the scholarship, religion, folklore and literature of the Middle Ages.

The chapter on medieval scholarship moves from early modern writers Conrad Gessner, Ulisse Aldrovandi, and Edward Topsell back to thirteenth-century thinkers Bartholomaeus Anglicus Thomas Cantimpré and Vincent of Beauvais, and the traditions of the *Hexameron*, *Physiologus* and the bestiary. Honegger familiarizes his readers with the dominance of scripture and *auctores*, the *liber naturae*, the *Physiologus's* organization into *natura* and *significatio*. Focus is on two seminal texts: Isidore of Seville's *Etymologiae*, where dragons are related to pagan mythology, and John Trevisa's fourteenth-century translation of Bartholomaeus Anglicus's *De proprietatibus rerum*, which revises and elaborates Bartholomaeus's original Latin. In both works, the dragon emerges "as a real though sometimes exotic and strange animal" (33).

Honegger's discussion of the dragon in medieval religion first surveys the scriptural and allegorical traditions. In a long section on saints, Honegger then discusses St. Michael and St. George as dragon slayers who resort to physical force. He identifies William Caxton's translation of Jacobus de Voragine's *Legenda aurea* as a text in which the Christian writer adapted the folktale of a dragon slayer into the life of St. George, turning St. George's vanquishing the dragon into a battle against pagan forces. He then discusses saints who use prayers and invocations to overcome dragons. Again resorting to Caxton's version, he discusses St. Margaret of Antioch's bursting from the dragon's belly as an example of typology, recalling Jonah and the whale and its prefiguring Christ's Harrowing of Hell. The dragon thus becomes integral to the saint's *imitatio Christi*. In a section on religious art, Honegger first reads *The Woman of the Apocalypse* (the so-called Morgan Apocalypse) from the mid-thirteenth century against its scriptural sources. The second analysis provides a fascinating look at a silk chasuble held at Lucerne from the fifteenth century on. Its back section depicts two Chinese dragons. While the origin of the vestment is shrouded in mystery, its afterlife illustrates a fascinating intercultural transfer. As Chinese dragons, unlike their Western relatives, are depicted positively and feature on ceremonial robes, they fit into no Western tradition. So the two exotic dragons spawned an aetiology first recorded by Renward Cysat in 1580 that made them part of Lucerne's history. Importantly, the dragons now exist in "a secular, non-religious framework where [they] were accepted as part of the local fauna and tradition" (60).

In chapter 3, Honegger treats the medieval dragon as a creature of folklore. As there is only little literary evidence of the folklore dragon, Honegger uses Tolkien's notion of the "Cauldron of Story," which contains a brew of motifs, characters, and plot elements that can be accessed and enriched by all tellers of tales, oral or literary, then and now. He puts Tolkien's theory to good use in a thorough reading of James Dacres Devlin's *The Mordiford Dragon* (1848), which contains variant versions, written and oral sources, as well as a critical discussion. The tale and its manifestations signpost key motifs of dragon narratives that point back to oral traditions (e.g., the dragon slayer's resorting to trickery), but also offer a first glimpse of ironic-parodistic treatments of dragons.

In the final chapter, Honegger turns to the most famous literary dragons. Section 1, "*Beowulf*—and Beyond," which is prefaced with a terse overview of the history and traditions of the poem, presents Beowulf's final opponent in insightful readings of well-selected passages. The author stresses that the detailed descriptions of the dragon relegate "any allegorical or symbolic meanings to second place" (87) and that the narrator embeds the dragon in the realities of Geatish life, thus advocating a tension between the Germanic and Christian layers of the narrative. He widens the perspective by looking at the Middle English romances *Sir Eglamour of Artois*, where the dragon has become the hero's traditional *maximum obstaculum*, and *Sir Degarée*, where the hero's clubbing the dragon to death reveals the comic potential of dragon combat. Section 2 presents *Bevis of Hampton*, which Honegger deems "the summa of medieval dragon lore" (112) because it harks back to all previous traditions and the elements associated with them. Looking at the poet's extensive description, Honegger reads the dragon as a composite creature that combines organic with nonorganic elements. As in *Beowulf*, the details in description overpower the allegorical significance of the beast. However, Bevis's battle against the monster takes a turn to the allegorical and becomes a figuration of man's fight against evil.

In a bare 120 pages of main text (barring the endnotes), Honegger's *Introducing the Medieval Dragon* covers all major authors and texts, and positions them in the varied traditions of the Middle Ages. The book benefits considerably from its dual-language approach, which offers the Old or Middle English original and its translation, while Latin texts are provided in the perceptive endnotes. This choice is especially commendable in a time when even highly specialized publications rarely offer original texts. As the book wears its learning lightly, it will appeal to a wide readership. University teachers will find Honegger a well-versed Cicerone, pointing out major motifs, concepts and backgrounds. The monograph succeeds in teaching readers to look at the dragon with, as it were, medieval eyes, as its focus lies firmly on the medieval worldview; e.g., it does not present postmodern trends and theories. The book's appeal is enhanced by Anke Eissmann's illustrations of famous dragon images and the annotated bibliography of select texts that precedes the bibliography proper and the index. The book is highly recommended for the university classroom, for students and for abecedarian researchers. It will also be read with pleasure and profit by connoisseurs.

Maik Goth
Ruhr-Universität Bochum
maik.goth@rub.de

Contesting Europe. Comparative Perspectives on Early Modern Discourses on Europe, 1400–1800. Edited by Nicolas Detering, Clementina Marsico, and Isabella Walser-Bürgler. Leiden: Brill, 2020. Pp. XVIII + 386.

Historians have for a long time been fascinated by how people in the past conceived of the region, country, or even continent where they lived. Examples include classic studies on nationalism and national identity, such as Benedict Anderson's *Imagined Communities: Reflections on the Origin and Spread of Nationalism* (London, 1983) and on the development of a European sense of identity, such as Denys Hay's *Europe: The Emergence of an Idea* (Edinburgh, 1957). The editors of this volume take the work of Burke and others as their starting point to contribute to our knowledge of early modern discourses on Europe by (a) moving beyond the select corpus of "canonical texts, which most of historical research on Europe has relied on"; (b) drawing a more "differentiated picture of these discourses based on a more varied selection of sources and issues"; (c) offering a comparative perspective on these discourses through the inclusion of material written in languages in which perhaps not all early modernists are fluent, such as the Slavic languages and Neo-Latin.

The essays in the volume have been divided across three sections. Summarizing all fifteen essays lies beyond the scope of this review, so what follows is a sketch of the overarching themes in each section. The first, "Embodying Europe," analyses discourses on Europe aiming to propagate (perceived) aspects of the continent through embodiments or allegories. Thus, the first essays by Nicolas Detering, Dennis Pulina, and Ronny Kaiser discuss several examples of *lamentationes*, literary denunciations or expressions of grief in either prose or poetry, usually with regard to contemporary events. The examples presented here decry the religious and political divisions in sixteenth-century Europe, which allowed the Ottoman Empire to expand inside the continent. The relationship between Europe and other continents is looked at from a visual perspective in the essays by, among others, Marion Romberg, who discusses allegorical depictions of the continents in parish churches in the southern Holy Roman Empire before 1800. Among other things, she demonstrates how from around 1700 such depictions moved from the restricted area of the choir to the laymen's area of the nave, suggesting that this development reflects how a European consciousness became more clearly part of "ordinary people's" lives.

Medievalia et Humanistica, New Series, Number 47 (Reinhold F. Glei and Maik Goth, eds.), Rowman & Littlefield, 2022.

The second section, "Centralising Europe," analyses discourses on elements, nations, and countries that were perceived as central or marginal in Europe. In her essay, Lucie Storchová presents a seventeenth-century polemic about the origins of the Bohemians: were they autochthonous to central Europe, or had they arrived from the east as descendants of the Sarmatians? Another example is the essay by Ovanes Akopyan, who compares European descriptions of Muscovy with Russian reflections on their relationship with (the rest of) Europe.

Finally, in the third section, "Balancing Europe," we find essays that "study the interplay between *plurality* (Europe and its parts) *and power* as it appears in metaphors of harmonious balance, fierce competition or feared slavery by a new hegemony" (5). A representative essay for this section is the one by Niels Grüne and Stefan Ehrenpreis. This essay discusses examples of how Europeans (often ambassadors) reflected on the way non-European states (e.g., the Ottoman and Mughal Empires) were run. For many of these diplomats—usually members of the European nobility—it was their ancient feudal rights that offered them protection from the kind of despotism that subjects of the Ottoman Sultan or Great Mughal had to contend with—regardless of their social status. The vestiges of medieval feudalism were therefore perceived as the basis of political freedom. Conversely, European monarchs like France's Louis XIV, who were perceived by their opponents as too despotic, were described in orientalizing terms.

Of course, the coverage of themes in an edited volume often depends on available contributors, their research interests, and their take on a particular topic. Therefore, there will undoubtedly be readers who feel that some important supranational elements that might have contributed to a growing sense of European awareness are underrepresented or not touched upon at all. The only essay, for example, that deals with the concept of the Republic of Letters is that by Enrico Zucchi, who looks at early eighteenth-century Italian journalism. It would have been interesting to see a case study on the interaction between the concept of the Republic of Letters and an emerging European consciousness in an earlier period. The *terminus ad quem* for the volume is 1800, but the eighteenth century is a little underrepresented compared to the sixteenth and seventeenth centuries. This is forgivable, even justified, because the volume was at least in part conceived as a response to Peter Burke's article "Did Europe Exist before 1700?"[1] Finally, as noted above, the editors and contributors make a sympathetic and convincing argument that scholars should pay more attention to source material in, e.g., Latin. This reviewer was therefore a little surprised that nowhere did he find that a discussion of the role played by Latin itself as opposed to the European national and regional vernaculars is explicitly considered. After all, in the early modern period, this language was a vestige of the time when much of Europe had been united in the Roman Empire and later in the Catholic Church; even after the Reformation, it long remained a lingua franca for learned international communication. The fact that authors who wrote in Latin rather than their native tongue did so in order to reach an international, European audience is implied, but never really looked at or analyzed. These observations aside, the essays in this volume are of excellent quality, and its usefulness is further increased by the fact that much previously unedited material has been added to the essays as appendices.

Note

1. P. Burke, "Did Europe Exist before 1700?," *History of European Ideas* 1 (1980), 21–29.

Floris Verhaart
University College Cork
fverhaart@ucc.ie

Walther Ludwig, *Florilegium Neolatinum: Ausgewählte Aufsätze 2014–2018.* Edited by Astrid Steiner-Weber (Noctes Neolatinae, 33). Hildesheim: Georg Olms, 2019. Pp. XII + 918, 26 illustrations.

Honor to whom honor is due—this does of course hold true for Walther Ludwig. As one of the pioneers of Neo-Latin studies, he has been shaping, exploring, and developing the field for decades. The *Florilegium Neolatinum* bears witness to his ongoing creative power. It was published on the occasion of Ludwig's ninetieth birthday and is the latest of four volumes containing his collected writings. After the *Miscella Neolatina* (2004/2005), the *Supplementa Neolatina* (2008) and the *Opuscula Historico-Philologica* (2014), the *Florilegium Neolatinum* now offers articles Ludwig published between 2014 and 2018, dealing with the Latin (partly also the Greek) literature from the sixteenth to the nineteenth century. In the most literal sense, one could thus say that Ludwig's achievements speak volumes.

The articles gathered in the *Florilegium Neolatinum* amount to twenty-six revised and partially extended reprints of articles previously published in collected volumes and journals. Furthermore, the collection presents five new articles and two additional contributions relating to Ludwig's biography, a "Prooemium" and "Epilog" that frame the book nicely. The added value of this volume—as always in such cases—is evident: First, the collective power of the articles assembled can serve as an effective working tool for Neo-Latin scholars. Second, the book demonstrates that Latin and Greek have been embedded in a historical continuum reaching from antiquity up to modernity. Finally, the articles provide an overview of the role and significance of Latin and Greek in the early modern period that is relevant for anyone interested in or working on early modern history and culture.

The volume is divided into four chapters: I) the sixteenth, II) the seventeenth, III) the eighteenth, and IV) the nineteenth century. Interestingly enough, the number of articles found in each of the chapters (ten in the first and second, five in the third, and six in the fourth chapter) seems to broadly reflect the natural scope of Neo-Latin literature. While it reached its peak in the sixteenth and seventeenth centuries, it loses significance in the eighteenth century, before it occasionally sparks interest in romantic or traditional distortions in the nineteenth century. At the end of the volume, the reader is supplied with twenty-six illustrations of early modern prints and medals, followed by a list of Ludwig's publications

Medievalia et Humanistica, New Series, Number 47 (Reinhold F. Glei and Maik Goth, eds.), Rowman & Littlefield, 2022.

from 2013 to 2018 (including a preview of his 2019 publications) and an index of names that has been put together by Ludwig himself.

Just to give an impression of Ludwig's remarkable service to the field of Neo-Latin studies: in geographical terms, the volume's respective articles relate to early modern humanism in Germany, Austria, the Netherlands, France, Britain, Spain, Italy, Bohemia, Poland, and Hungary. The topics cover both the Catholic and the Lutheran traditions. The thematic setting includes educational and philosophical history, the history of the book, and the history of ideas. The genres discussed range from declamations, emblems, epigrams, letters, medals, and historiographical writings to autobiographies, travel literature, dramas, family albums, satires, and smaller poetry. At the center of the articles, one may find both prominent figures (e.g., Philip Melanchthon, Laurentius Rhodomanus, Justus Lipsius) and less known authors (e.g., Georg Wilhelm Prahmer, Joseph Lang, several nineteenth-century poets from Württemberg).

The two framing contributions, the proem and the epilogue, specify Ludwig's achievements. The proem serves as a perfect introduction to a jubilee volume dedicated to a man of letters like Ludwig, as it offers the continuation of the *Testimonia amoris librorum* begun in 2008 and developed in 2014 (nos. 1–18). This time, the *Testimonia* (nos. 19–27) relate to Latin, English, French, and German expressions for the love of books from the sixteenth to the nineteenth centuries. Among them (no. 26) there is even mention of one of Ludwig's ancestors himself, the scholar Johann Peter von Lud(e)wig (1668–1743), to whom Ludwig also refers in the epilogue of the volume. This epilogue reproduces the words of thanks Ludwig gave at the University of Vienna in January 2016 after being awarded the university's honorary doctorate.

The five articles Ludwig published for the first time in this volume illustrate as broad an interest as the rest of the chapters. Article I.10 makes an important contribution to the study of networks and career building in sixteenth-century learned circles by presenting unknown letters by Justus Lipsius, David Chytraeus, or Martin Crusius to the statesman Heinrich Rantzau (pp. 287–310); article II.5 offers new insights into the Jesuit teaching of Horace and how the Jesuits coped with pagan or obscene passages (pp. 399–433); article III.4 corrects the wrong translation of the motto *Provide et constanter* of Charles Eugene, Duke of Württemberg, based on Tacitus's description of Emperor Tiberius (pp. 713–18); article IV.5 examines a French medal awarded on the occasion of composing Latin poetry in 1822 and a Bavarian medal celebrating Jakob Balde from 1828 (pp. 849–50); article IV.6 looks at Greek quotations in medals awarded to nineteenth-century philologists (pp. 851–54).

In sum, the *Florilegium Neolatinum* presents another splendid collection of Walther Ludwig's works, which cannot only be considered, in some ways, as a history of Neo-Latin literature *in nuce*, but will also incite many other scholars in the field to elaborate on Ludwig's findings.

Isabella Walser-Bürgler
Ludwig Boltzmann Institute for Neo-Latin Studies, Innsbruck
isabella.walser@neolatin.lbg.ac.at

Gender, Health, and Healing, 1250–1550. Edited by Sara Ritchey and Sharon Strocchia.
Amsterdam: Amsterdam University Press, 2020. Pp. 330.

The eleven essays collected in *Gender, Health, and Healing, 1250–1550*,
as Naama Cohen-Hanegbi highlights in her afterword to the volume,
make a substantial contribution to our understanding of "women's
health" and "women's roles in healthcare" (316) in both northern
Europe and the Mediterranean, as well as in Christian and Islamicate
contexts. Academic and professional medicine in the medieval and
early modern periods very often marginalizes women, their bodies,
and experiences, as well as their knowledge and varied roles in healthcare and healing—as does the research devoted to it. As Sara Ritchey
and Sharon Strocchia set out in their introduction, however, a turn to
vernacular household medicine; to the intersection of medicine and
culture—particularly of "household medicine and spiritual-liturgical
therapeutics"; to everyday practice; to care (rather than cure); and to
material culture enable instead a decentering of "theoretical medicine
to make room for the lived experience of healthcare in all its diversity"
(15). In so doing, these essays together persuasively show the authority
and knowledge of women (as mothers, daughters, neighbors, servants,
etc.) in organizing and performing healthcare "within the domestic
realm and beyond" (16). Two areas on which the volume focuses,
household medicine, on the one hand, and "care things" (to take up
Cordula Nolte's phrase, 216), on the other, emerge as especially powerful not only as tools for recovering women's health and healing but
also as methods for interdisciplinary study, which reaches across and
between medical, religious, and literary cultures.

The collection expands our understanding of particular gendered
health problems through examining, for example, new or neglected
sources and by making available translations of them in essays on
breastbleeding (Monserrat Cabré and Fernando Salmón); breast care
and breastfeeding (Belle S. Tuten); menstruation, conception, and re-
production (Julia Gruman Martins); infertility and old age (Catherine
Rider); and gynecological practice (Sara Verskin).

Many of the sources drawn on in the essays can be described as
"hybrid"—that is, as bridging between either academic and household
contexts or medical and religious domains. For example, three sources
stemming from Italy in the fifteenth and sixteenth centuries—the

Medievalia et Humanistica, New Series, Number 47 (Reinhold F. Glei and Maik Goth,
eds.), Rowman & Littlefield, 2022.

Tractatus de passionibus mamillarum (Tuten), Caterina Sforza's household recipe book (Sheila Barker and Strocchia), and the *Dificio di ricette* (Martins)—share in learned medical knowledge but are clearly associated with vernacular, household, and female readership. The two recipe books, moreover, further demonstrate the role of women not only in providing care within household contexts but also in empirical investigation—in testing recipes (see, e.g., 140, 167), and in transmitting and authoring medical knowledge.

A further three sources—the biblical proverb recorded in Sirach 36.27 ("Ubi non est mulier, ingemiscit egens?") and circulating in "conduct manuals, hospital ordinances, works of literature, and rhetorical tracts" (Eva-Maria Cersovsky, 191–92); the Psalter-hours preserved as Liège, Bibliothèque de l'Université MS 431 (Ritchey); and the shrine and relics of St. Cunigunde (Iliana Kandzha)—would more typically be categorized as sacred, biblical, or liturgical. In this collection, however, they are shown to be implicated in "spiritual-liturgical therapeutics" and in shaping understandings of women as agents of health and care. Especially striking, the Liège Psalter-hours and St. Cunigunde's relics, along with bathtubs (Ayman Yasin Atat) and beds (Nolte), compose the volume's path-breaking exploration of "care things" and therapeutic tools. Ritchey's essay, for instance, through the specific example of MS 431's association with what she terms "women's circuits of care" (in the *beguinage* of St. Christopher's and the hospitals and leprosarium connected with it), demonstrates how psalters—used in a combination of prayer and liturgical performance, and at "the bedsides of the sick, the parturient, and the dying"—could "structure therapeutic interactions and accrue therapeutic significance" (43–44). Utilizing the written and visual evidence of a sixteenth-century commentary on herniotomy by Caspar Stromayr, Nolte also takes up "object-centred analyses" to offer an experimental reading of "premodern 'care choreography'" (216), which considers both the "material environments, and spatial arrangements of bodies" (217), cared for within domestic spaces, in order to bring into nearer view both the "collaborative nature of domestic care" (238) and the medical agency of women within it.

An important contribution to scholarship that aims to recover medical knowledge, subjects, agents, and experiences from the margins, *Gender, Health, and Healing* is also valuable for the methodologies it adopts and innovates. In her closing remarks, Cohen-Hanegbi observes that the "potential avenues for retelling the history of medicine" mapped out by the volume require "narratives that bridge disciplines, geographies, and faith traditions; they must be more integrative and inclusive" (323). *Gender, Health, and Healing* shows persuasively how and why to do this for a history of gender; but in so doing treads a path for future medieval and early modern scholarship more broadly.

Katie L. Walter
University of Sussex
K.L.Walter@sussex.ac.uk

Books for Review

Jacob M. Baum, *Reformation of the Senses: The Paradox of Religious Belief and Practice in Germany*. Studies in Sensory History. Urbana: University of Illinois Press, 2018. Pp. ix + 296, 4 b/w ill., 3 b/w tables.

Guillaume Bonnet, ed., *Jean-Baptiste Santeul: Œvre poétique complète*. Tome I. Bibliothèque du XVIIᵉ siècle 31, Série *Voix poétiques* 6. Paris: Classiques Garnier, 2019. Pp. 619.

Guillaume Bonnet, ed., *Jean-Baptiste Santeul: Œvre poétique complète*. Tome I. Bibliothèque du XVIIᵉ siècle 32, Série *Voix poétiques* 7. Paris: Classiques Garnier, 2019. Pp. 1719, 10 b/w ill.

Bryan Brazeau, ed., *The Reception of Aristotle's* Poetics *in the Italian Renaissance and Beyond: New Directions in Criticism*. Bloomsbury Studies in the Aristotelian Tradition. London et al.: Bloomsbury Academic, 2020. Pp. xii + 299, 11 b/w ill.

John Bugbee, *God's Patients: Chaucer, Agency, and the Nature of Laws*. Notre Dame, IN: University of Notre Dame Press, 2019. Pp. xxii + 477.

Michael Cichon and Yin Liu, eds., *Proverbia Septentrionalia: Essays on Proverbs in Medieval Scandinavian and English Literature*. Medieval and Renaissance Texts and Studies 542. Tempe, AZ: ACMRS, 2019. Pp. vii + 216.

Mark Cruse, ed., *Performance and Theatricality in the Middle Ages and the Renaissance*. Arizona Studies in the Middle Ages and the Renaissance 41. Turnhout: Brepols, 2018. Pp. xiii + 207, 23 b/w ill., 1 b/w table.

Joachim Knape, *Rhetorik als Komplementärethik: Georg Greflingers Ethica Complementoria 1643: Text und Untersuchung*. Gratia 66. Wiesbaden: Harrasowitz Verlag, 2020. Pp. vi + 158, 1 b/w ill.

James C. Kriesel, *Bocaccio's Corpus: Allegory, Ethics, and Vernacularity*. The William and Katherine Devers Series in Dante and Medieval Italian Literature 15. Notre Dame, IN: University of Notre Dame Press, 2019. Pp. xvii + 381.

Rebecca Lemon, *Addiction and Devotion in Early Modern England*. Haney Foundation Series. Philadelphia: University of Pennsylvania Press, 2018. Pp. xv + 258.

Diane J. Reilly, *The Cistercian Reform and the Art of the Book in Twelfth-Century France*. Knowledge Communities. Amsterdam: Amsterdam University Press, 2018. Pp. XVI + 229, 16 color plates, 20 b/w ill., 5 b/w tables.

Catherine Sanok, *New Legends of England: Forms of Community in Late Medieval Saints' Lives*. The Middle Ages Series. Philadelphia: University of Pennsylvania Press, 2018. Pp. 349, 8 b/w ill.

Charles Russell Stone, *The* Roman de toute chevalerie*: Reading Alexander Romance in Late Medieval England*. Toronto et al.: University of Toronto Press, 2019. Pp. xii + 255.

Medievalia et Humanistica, New Series, Number 47 (Reinhold F. Glei and Maik Goth, eds.), Rowman & Littlefield, 2022.

Christine Thumm, *Erzählen und Überzeugen: Rhetorischer Impetus protestantischer Literatur bei Kaspar Goldtwurm (1524–1559) im Zeitalter der Konfessionalisierung.* Gratia 65. Wiesbaden: Harrassowitz Verlag, 2020. Pp. vii + 398, 7 b/w ill.

Pier Mattia Tommasino, *The Venetian Qur'an: A Renaissance Companion to Islam.* Translated by Sylvia Notini. Material Texts. Philadelphia: University of Pennsylvania Press, 2018. Pp. xix + 297.